The World News Prism

The World News Prism

SECOND EDITION

CHANGING MEDIA, CLASHING IDEOLOGIES

William A. Hachten
With the collaboration of Harva Hachten

 Iowa State University Press / Ames

WILLIAM A. HACHTEN is professor of journalism and mass communication at the University of Wisconsin-Madison. He served as director of its School of Journalism and Mass Communication from 1975 to 1980. His earlier books include *Muffled Drums: The News Media in Africa* and *The Supreme Court on Freedom of the Press,* both published by Iowa State University Press, *Mass Communication in Africa: An Annotated Bibliography,* and, in 1984, *The Press and Apartheid: Repression and Propaganda in South Africa,* co-authored with C. Anthony Giffard.

© 1981, 1987   Iowa State University Press, Ames, Iowa 50010
All rights reserved

Composed by Iowa State University Press
Printed in the United States of America

First edition, 1981
     Second printing, 1982
     Third printing, 1983
     Fourth printing, 1986
Second edition, 1987

Library of Congress Cataloging-in-Publication Data

Hachten, William A.
     The world news prism.

     Bibliography: p.
     Includes index.
     1. Foreign news.   2. Communication, International.   3. Journalism — Political aspects.   I. Hachten, Harva.   II. Title.
PN4784.F6H3   1987   070.4'33   87–3845
ISBN 0–8138–1579–7

TO THE MEMORY OF

My Mother and My Father

Contents

Preface

$\mathbf{M}$UCH has happened in international news communication since the first edition of this book was published in 1981, most dramatically in technological developments and utilization of new and old communications hardware. Across the Northern Hemisphere, applications of communications satellites have proliferated. Direct broadcasting from portable transmitters to satellites, then back to dish antennas — bypassing complicated, expensive ground installations — has become commonplace.

Small, portable earth terminals, for example, enabled broadcasters reporting the fall of the Marcos government in the Philippines to send their television reports directly to the Intelsat system and thus to the whole world. Or a Pan Am jetliner hijacked in Karachi, Pakistan, instantly becomes a global "media event," riveting millions to their television screens to watch live the drama unfold to a bloody resolution.

In the ideological arena, controversies between North and South over news values and issues have quieted somewhat but have not gone away. Advocates of a New World Information Order remain convinced of the rightness of their cause. Differing philosophies of journalism still clash in the world's news centers.

For this second edition the text has been thoroughly revised and expanded, with new material added in every section. I have also added one new chapter, "Polishing the Prism: Public Diplomacy and Propaganda," which covers international radio and efforts of governments to influence world opinion and manipulate foreign news media.

As before, this overview of trends and developments in international news is primarily intended as a text for students in journalism and communications programs who are concerned with how news is gathered and moves about the world. I would hope that their teachers as well as journalists and others will also find this book of some interest.

In this information age, communications systems and technologies are at the leading edge of social, economic, and scientific change. With the unprecedented growth in global telecommunications, the public has developed a more immediate concern with both how world news is collected and disseminated and the symbiotic relationship between events and those who report them.

I am again indebted to John McNelly for his valuable suggestions and to Betty McClurkin for her careful editing. Most helpful, as before, was my wife, Harva Hachten, who as my collaborator edited the manuscript carefully and rewrote parts of it. I am fortunate to be married to a writer who shares my interest in international communication and knows how to write. I alone am responsible for the judgments and any errors in the book.

W. A. H.

Introduction

ON an August day in 1969, an estimated 600 million people throughout the world watched Neil Armstrong take man's first walk on the moon. They sat in front of their television sets not as Americans, Frenchmen, Africans, or Japanese, but as earthlings watching in awe as one of their kind first stepped onto another planet.

Almost thirteen years later another space event riveted viewers around the world to their television sets. This time the emotion was not awe but fascinated horror as the space shuttle *Challenger* exploded in 1986 shortly after lift-off, killing all seven crew members. Millions around the world watched live and countless replays of the fiery end of the craft—the sudden fireball billowing into great trails of white smoke that left a tragically beautiful image in the bright blue January sky. The fact that the disaster occurred within television camera range highlighted that medium's ability to enable all of us anywhere to share events of great import with an impact unattainable with the printed word. This, as a *New York Times* editorial put it, "offers a frontier of human perceptions fully as challenging as the frontier of space."

These quintessential media events vividly illustrate the "technetronic" age, the melding of technology and electronics, that planet earth has entered—a new era whose potential we but dimly perceive, whose complicated gadgetry only few of us totally grasp, whose social, political, and economic consequences are accelerating change and cleavages among the nations of the world.

For the world we live in today is changing rapidly, in no small part because worldwide television, communications satellites (comsats), high-speed transmission of news and data, and other computer and electronic hardware and software have transformed the ways that nations and peoples communicate with one another. The fact that a news event can be transmitted almost instantaneously to newsrooms and onto television screens around the world can be as important as the event itself. Long-distance mass communications has become a rudimentary central nervous system for our fragile, shrinking, and increasingly interdependent world.

This book describes and analyzes the dramatically altered role of today's transnational news media in our evolving technetronic age. On the one hand are the technological and operational changes taking place in the international news media, with their enhanced capability for global communication that is reshaping "spaceship earth." On the other hand are the frictions and problems these changes have wrought, most notably the conflicts over transnational news gathering and dissemination and the worldwide impact of television programming, motion pictures, videos, radio broadcasting, and other aspects of mass culture, much of it coming out of the United States.

Unquestionably, the current clashes and disputes over international communication between the West, the Socialist nations, and the Third World are serious and disturbing. Such catch phrases as "free flow of information," "media imperialism," and "new world information order" suggest the profound ideological and political differences over the ways the global news media should be organized and controlled.

The concern here is with the many facets of this change and their effects on transnational journalism and mass communication. This book is intended to provide some insights into how and why international news communication is evolving and where it is headed.

Few of us can appreciate, much less fully understand, the meaning of the global information revolution we are living through, a revolution that has enveloped us virtually unnoticed. The major artifacts of this quiet revolution are the computer and the communications satellite — sophisticated electronic devices that have become as much a part of our lives as the electric light.

Journalism and mass communication recently have made quantum leaps in scope and reach because of application of this new technology to the gathering, production, and dissemination of news throughout the globe.

We may not be aware of how our perceptions of the world are changed by the transformed news system, but we quickly learn to take that system for granted. If there is another seizure of American hostages during the hijacking of an airliner or cruise ship, or a new outbreak of warfare in the Middle East, or a coup d'etat in Africa, we expect to see live television reports the same day or on twenty-four-hour news stations within the same hour, via satellite. We are fascinated but not surprised to see detailed, computer-refined pictures of Uranus or Halley's comet or the wreckage of the Titanic on the floor of the Atlantic three miles down. We no longer wonder that we and most of the world can watch the Olympic games on television every four years from half a world away.

In a broader context, the fact that information of all kinds, including urgent news, can now be communicated almost instantly to almost anywhere has profound implications for international organization and interaction. To grasp fully what is happening all around us, we must modify our ways of looking at the world and our place in it. We need new perceptions of international communication and its potential to shape and direct the world's changes and adjustments during the remaining years of the twentieth century.

Inexorably, a new global society of sorts is emerging, and the media of mass communication, along with the global telecommunications and air transportation, are providing the essential linkages that make interaction and cooperation—and frictions— possible. Full understanding of the nature of this new society requires that today's students of international communication be conversant with world affairs, including recent history, and able to recognize and understand significant trends as they are occurring. Further, they must keep up with technological innovations in communication media and journalistic practices. (Comsats are just one example of the truly revolutionary impact that communications technology has had on the modern world. The earlier role of transistor radios in the Third World is another example. In many ways the modern world is itself a product of our greatly enhanced ability to communicate.) Finally, students of international communication must be attuned to the roles and functions of mass communication in changing the political and social relationships of the world's peoples.

The interplay of these three elements makes the study of international communications fascinating and important. The major emphasis throughout this book is on the journalistic aspects of international communication—the new challenges and perils of reporting the news, the important but imperfect and controversial ways that journalists and mass communicators keep the world informed.

Several chapters concern the changing media—the ways that international journalism is adapting to altering global conditions and utilizing the new hardware of our information age. Some of the fundamental changes that are bringing all peoples of the world—for better or worse—much closer together are broadly outlined.

Today, for the first time in history, all nations, however remote, have stepped onto the stage of modern world history. What happens in Uganda or Indonesia has global meaning and often sends repercussions around the world, in part because events there are reported. But more important, a degree of interdependence among all peoples and nations has developed that never existed before. Americans, perhaps, are much slower than others to recognize this. Since our families, jobs, and local communities are of primary and immediate concern, most people, including many leaders, do not perceive the rapid and fundamental changes taking place, changes directly related to our expanded powers of long-distance communication.

For the world has been evolving an international news system that moves information and mass culture ever faster and in greater volume to any place on earth where an antenna can be put up on a shortwave radio or a dish antenna installed to receive television programs from a communications satellite. Although politics, economic disparities, cultural and linguistic differences, and ideology keep us apart on most issues, the international news system has on occasion made us one community, if only for a few brief moments—as when Neil Armstrong took that "one giant leap for mankind" or the reality of the *Challenger* tragedy was etched in the smoke patterns in the sky.

Actually, the reportage of Armstrong's walk has further relevance to this book because the new information age is partly an outgrowth of the exploration of space. The comsat high-speed data transmission, and sophisticated computer technology are by-products of space technology, and all are playing integral roles in the transformation of international communication and transnational journalism.

The modern world's practice of collecting and distributing news is only about a hundred years old and was initiated by news agencies of the United States and the great imperial powers, Britain and France. Today, the world agencies—the Associated Press and United Press International (U.S.), Reuters (Britain), and Agence France Presse (France)—are still the principal but not the only conduits of transnational news, although they and other media have been transformed by the new space-age technology.

Change has been coming so quickly that it is often difficult to stay current with the ways news is being moved. And to understand the future potential of these space-age gadgets is like trying to perceive in 1905 what the absurd horseless carriage would do in time to the cities and life-styles of the twentieth century.

Furthermore, technology is modifying some of the institutions of transnational communication. Subtly and almost imperceptibly, various media, especially the major news agencies, are evolving from national to increasingly international, or better, supranational, institutions of mass communication. The highly successful *International Herald Tribune* reaches a sophisticated non-American readership; *Time* and *Newsweek* publish special editions truly international in outlook; the *Asian Wall Street Journal* is widely read by Asian businessmen and women. This trend may be controversial, but there is no doubt that it is happening as a response to the needs of a shrinking world. Concomitantly, English is evolving into the world's media language. The logic of mass communication requires that sender and receiver understand a common language, and so far, English, the language of science and technology—and computers—is it.

Modern media, especially shortwave radio, are utilized by many nations for purposes of "international political communication"—a polite term for propaganda. The international broadcasters—BBC World Service, Voice of America, Radio Moscow, Deutsche Welle, Radio Cairo, and many others, including small Third World national services—use radio to project their interpretations and reactions to world events. "Propaganda warfare" appears in a variety of manifestations of international politics.

The international news media, furthermore, are unevenly distributed among nations, a reality that has created serious frictions between the haves and have-nots in mass communication. Moreover, the explosion of communications technology has coincided with the post–World War II decolonization of the Third World, and the penetration of Western news and mass culture into the newly independent nations has been perceived by some as a new attempt to reassert the domination of the former colonial powers.

Part of this book focuses on the differences that frustrate and at times inhibit the flow of international news and divide journalists and mass communicators: political and ideological differences, economic disparities, geographic and ethnic divisions.

The conflicts and frictions in international communication arise from divergent concepts of mass communication. In the concept of the press that has evolved in Western democratic nations, which dominate international news flow, the journalist and the press are relatively independent of government, free to report directly to the public that uses the information to understand the world and assess its governors. This view is unacceptable to Communist nations, which, following the teachings of Lenin, have placed their media fully within the governmental structure to better serve the goals of the state. In the numerous, mostly impoverished nations of the Third World (neither Western nor Communist), a similar theory—the Developmental concept— has been emerging, which holds that mass media must be mobilized to serve the goals of nation building and economic development.

The clashes between these concepts and various debates on controls on the flow of news have been reverberating in recent years through international organizations such as the United Nations Educational, Scientific and Cultural Organization (UNESCO) and international professional media groups such as the International Press Institute and the Inter American Press Association. (The decisions of the United States, and later Britain and Singapore, to withdraw from UNESCO were directly related to the international news controversies.) Although efforts to reconcile these conflicting approaches to mass communication have been slow and painful, an accommodation is necessary for world understanding and harmony. Western journalists believe strongly that

their ability to gather news abroad is becoming increasingly im-
paired as some Third World and Socialist nations frustrate and
block the activities of foreign reporters. Authoritarian governments with controlled press systems resent what they consider to be
the negative reporting of Western media and, as a result, do not
permit foreign reporters to enter. For their part, many non-Western
nations resent what they consider to be the domination of the
world news flow by a few Western news media. They see a kind of
"media imperialism" imposing alien values on developing societies
through a one-way flow of news. This monopolistic concentration
of the power to communicate, they say, does not serve the aspira-
tions of the many poor nations of the Third World.

The deep differences between the media-rich and media-poor
nations reflect closely other differences between rich and poor nations. Despite the impressive gains in the technical ability to communicate more widely and quickly, the disturbing evidence is that
the world in some ways may be growing further apart rather than
closer together. Technological change in communication seems to
race far ahead of our political skills to use it for the greatest good
of all.

The world's system of distributing news can be likened to a
crystal prism. What in one place is considered the straight white
light of truth travels through the prism and is refracted and bent
into a variety of colors and shades. One person's truth becomes to
another, biased reporting or propaganda, depending on where the
light strikes the prism and where it emerges. As we understand and
accept the optics of a prism for measuring the spectrum of light, so
must we understand and accept the transecting planes of different
cultural and political traditions that refract divergent perceptions
of our world.

At this point, I must acknowledge how the light refracts for
me. In considering the problems of international communications,
I have tried to be sympathetic to the views and frustrations of non-
Western nations and the enormous difficulties they face.

Journalism is a highly subjective pursuit, tempered and
shaped by the political conditions and cultural traditions of the
particular societies where it is practiced; the news and the world do
look different from Moscow, Lagos, or Jakarta than they do from
New York or London.

As a product of the Western press tradition, I believe journalists should be suspicious of and disagree at times with political leaders and with other journalists and the owners of the media. For me, the essence of journalism is diversity of ideas and the freedom to express them. I find it difficult to disagree with Albert Camus, who wrote that "a free press can of course be good or bad, but certainly without freedom, it will never be anything but bad. . . . Freedom is nothing else but a chance to be better, whereas enslavement is a certainty of the worse."

And in the dangerous, strife-ridden world of the late twentieth century, the billions of people inhabiting this planet deserve to know more about the events that affect their lives and well-being. Only journalists who are free and independent of authoritarian controls and other constraints can begin the difficult task of reporting the news and information we all need to know.

The World News Prism

1
Communication for an Interdependent World

By every indication the global human society is entering a period of change of historical proportions. Some call it the era of limited resources; some see it as the start of the new world economic order; some call it the communications age, or the post industrial society or the information age; but nearly every discipline and sector of society senses the shift taking place. By whatever name, . . . we are moving along a trajectory leading to a global human culture in which events across the world affect us with the same speed and impact as if they happened next door.

—Congressman George E. Brown
(D-California)

PERHAPS one of the most significant photographs of modern times was taken during the *Apollo 11* mission to the moon. The astronauts photographed the earthrise as seen from the moon, and there was our planet, like a big, cloudy, blue, agate marble. The widely reprinted picture illuminated the fragility and cosmic insignificance of our spaceship earth.

That stunning photograph coincided with the worldwide concern about ecology and global pollution; even more, it made it easy to grasp why many scientists already treat that cloudy, blue marble as a complete biological system in which change in one part will inevitably affect other parts.

Certainly, in the years since, concerned persons around the world have become more aware of our global interdependence. The great historical reality of our times is that the world is becoming a single, rudimentary community – with all that that implies. Today's world is faced with urgent and complex problems, most of them interrelated: overpopulation, poverty, famine, depletion of natural (especially energy) resources, pollution of the biosphere, the nuclear threat of the arms buildup, the widening gap between the rich and poor nations.

Although these problems may be found in some places and not in others, they are truly international in scope, and amelioration, much less solution, of any of them requires cooperation and goodwill among nations. And before that, there must be information and understanding of these challenges, for these are crises of interdependence. No one nation or even combination of nations can deal effectively with such global concerns as international monetary crises, pollution of the air and oceans, terrorism and hijacking of jet airliners, or widespread famine and food shortages. Yet the blinders of nationalism and modern tribalism continue to influence political leaders everywhere to react to international problems with narrow and parochial responses.

Few recent events illustrate this modern dilemma more vividly than the accident at the Chernobyl nuclear station near Kiev in late April 1986. Radiation levels rose significantly, first in Scandinavia and Eastern Europe and then in parts of Western Europe, contaminating crops and milk. People in the affected areas outside the Soviet Union demanded full information and were outraged when the Soviet government, for parochial reasons, at first tried to minimize the accident and then withheld details about the exact readings and extent of radiation contamination. But nuclear accidents of this scope are truly international catastrophes in which the fullest sharing of reliable information – news – to all people affected is the first requisite.

Lester Brown, an authority on global needs, has described the problems of the late twentieth century as "unique in their scale." Previous catastrophes – famines, floods, earthquakes, volcanic eruptions – were local and temporary. But now, the world's more pressing concerns can be solved only through multinational or global cooperation, and yet the institutions to cope with them are largely national. And since each technological innovation seems to create new problems but not the institutions capable of resolving them, Brown sees global conditions worsening in the years immediately ahead.

"Given the scale and complexity of these problems, the remainder of the twentieth century will at best be a traumatic period for mankind, even with a frontal attack on the principal threats to human well-being," Brown wrote. "At worst it will be catastrophic. At issue is whether we can grasp the nature and dimensions of the emerging threats to our well-being, whether we can create an integrated global economy and a workable world order, and whether we can reorder global priorities so that the quality of life will improve rather than deteriorate."[1]

Brown's view of world problems, shared by people in many countries, is still not understood by any great numbers of them. We Americans, for example, periodically turn inward and become self-absorbed, failing to comprehend how domestic problems have roots in events that occur thousands of miles away.

Historically, the interest of Americans in world events has ebbed and flowed, but events in the 1980s sharply reawakened Americans' interest in foreign affairs. The long ordeal of the kidnapped hostages at the American embassy in Iran, the Soviet incursion into Afghanistan, the chaotic violence of Lebanon and the ordeal of the hostages taken from the hijacked TWA airliner in Beirut, and terrorist attacks on airports in Rome and Vienna altered American public opinion sharply.

Furthermore, the soaring debts of Third World nations brought home another lesson in global interdependence to Americans. Latin American nations alone owed $360 billion ($100 billion by Mexico alone) to Western lenders, many of them American banks. And with numerous failures in the mid-1980s of U.S. banks—many carrying overseas loans—many Americans wondered about the safety of their personal savings.

Lester Brown pointed out that deficits of many kinds plagued the world in 1986. "We have begun to recognize," he wrote, "that Third World debts are not exclusively a Third World concern, and that solutions will require a partnership of debtors and creditors. Another key point needs to be acknowledged—that many fiscal, ecological, and social debts we incur today come at our children's expense. We can begin to retire our debts by recognizing that policies that take seriously the interests of the next generation usually best serve the current generation as well."[2]

Americans and some Third World leaders are becoming aware that population growth is putting intolerable pressures on the earth's land, water, and energy resources. Population Reference Bureau projections predict the world's population will be over 10.4 billion by the year 2100, which is more than double the 4.9 billion of the mid-1980s and more than five times the 2.5 billion people in the world in 1950. By the year 2025, 3.4 billion people are expected to be added to the world's population, 3.1 billion of them in Africa, Asia, and Latin America.

Thomas Merrick, president of the Population Reference Bureau, a private, nonprofit group, said, "For the developing nations it is a question of whether they will evolve into a kind of permanent underclass at the bottom of a two-tiered world economy. For the more developed nations, now approaching population stabilization, it may be difficult to continue to be islands of prosperity in a sea of poverty in a world made smaller by modern transportation and communication."[3] This separation will be more difficult to maintain if these imbalances generate waves of immigration.

Projections to 2100 indicate that India will become the world's most populous nation, with 1.63 billion, and China second, with 1.57 billion. Nigeria is expected to grow from 105.5 million (8th in the world) to 508.9 million people in 2100, which would make it the third largest nation on earth.

But even without these ominous developments, the very nature of the problems of the late twentieth century—transnational in scope and beyond the ability of this or any single nation to solve by itself—may be changing America's traditional provincialism.

The world's political structures, many believe, must be reshaped to enable us to cope with these global challenges; hence, the great importance, despite their serious shortcomings, of international organizations such as the United Nations and its attendant agencies.

Professor Edwin Reischauer, former U.S. ambassador to Japan, felt the response to the problem must start by changing individuals through a profound reshaping of education. Proliferating technology is fast destroying the cushioning that once existed between the different nations and cultures of the world. This in turn rapidly increases not only interdependence, but tensions as well.

"While the world is in the process of becoming a single great mass of humanity—a global community, as it is sometimes called," Reischauer wrote, "the very diverse national and cultural groupings that make up the world's population retain attitudes and habits more appropriate to a different technological age."

In the United States, he said, education "is not moving rapidly enough in the right directions to produce the knowledge about the outside world and the attitudes toward other peoples that may be essential for human survival within a generation or two. This I feel, is a much greater international problem than the military balance of power that absorbs so much of our attention today."[4]

Public opinion polls show that many Americans are uninformed about international affairs. For example, a Gallup Poll found that half of all Americans did not know that the United States had to import petroleum to meet its needs.

Few Americans, compared to Europeans, know foreign languages. A Presidential Commission on Foreign Language and International Studies concluded that "America's scandalous incompetence in foreign languages . . . explains our dangerously inadequate understanding of world affairs." And the situation is getting worse. In 1965, only one high school student in four studied a foreign language; at the end of the 1970s, the figure was one in seven. For 1984–85, about half the baccalaureate colleges and about four in ten of comprehensive and doctoral institutions had foreign language requirements for undergraduates. Very few however, required students to pass proficiency examinations, and a number allowed substitutions, such as computer courses, for the foreign language requirements.[5]

Professor Robert Ward has described the extent of our current neglect of international education at all levels as shocking. He might have added that most American news media pay far too little attention to news from abroad. What worries experts in this field is that ignorance and apathy about the world beyond America's borders may undermine this country's political, diplomatic, and economic influence. The next generation of Americans will be ill-prepared to grapple with global problems.

As important as formal education is, its influence sometimes does not change attitudes or improve understanding until a generation or two has passed. In immediate terms, the flow of information and news throughout the globe will have a greater impact than education on the world's ability to understand its problems and dangers.

Since World War II, an intricate and worldwide network of international news media has evolved, providing an expanded capability for information flows. This relationship between the capacity and the need to communicate rapidly has resulted from the interaction of two long-term historical processes: the evolution toward a single global society and the movement of civilization beyond four great benchmarks of human communication—speech, writing, printing, electronic communications (telephone and radio)—into a fifth era of long-distance instant communication based on communications satellites and computer technology.

Harold Lasswell believed that the mass media revolution has accelerated the tempo and direction of world history. What would have happened later has happened sooner, and changes in timing may have modified substantive development.[6]

The toppling of President Ferdinand Marcos from power in the Philippines in February 1986 provided a cogent example of the power of international news media to influence international politics. From the assassination of opposition leader Benigno Aquino through the election campaign, the U.S. media took a close interest in Marcos's affairs, reporting extensively on his "hidden wealth," including New York City real estate, as well as his dubious war record. This scrutiny helped the cause of candidate Corazon Aquino and galvanized U.S. public opinion and the Congress. The Reagan White House, in turn, was pushed to urge Marcos to step down after full media glare showed his election victory to be a fraud.

As Thomas Griffith of *Time* wrote, "The visuals on American TV did Marcos in. It wasn't Dan Rather or George Will. It was the pictures—the nuns, and the crowds wearing a touch of yellow, blocking the path of the armored cars. It was the sight of ballot boxes being dumped. In a few precarious days, it was the total collapse of Marcos's American support that sped the end. TV proved its awesome power."[7]

Commenting on the episode, Walter B. Wriston observed, "This is a brand new situation in the world. The global electronic network that has evolved in the last decade is forcing us to redefine our ideas of sovereignty. The rapid transmission of information has become a radical force for change, encouraging the growth of political and economic freedom. Marcos's demise is not an isolated instance."[8]

In another example, the world's reactions to the widespread racial conflict and state of emergency in South Africa during 1985–86 was greatly accelerated by the intense news coverage abroad. In 1960, after police killed 69 blacks and injured 180 others at the Sharpeville township, similar reactions to the imposition of martial law, continued racial unrest, worldwide condemnation, and flight of capital occurred. But in the mid-1980s, the foreign reactions—including protests and widespread condemnation, the imposition of sanctions, and the flight of capital—were much faster and more intense because the world was now seeing nightly color television reports of black protesters being attacked by white soldiers and police. Not surprisingly, South Africa in November 1985 banned all foreign photographic coverage by television and news photographers reporting racial violence in black townships. U.S. television coverage fell markedly after visuals were no longer available, and international pressures in South Africa lessened— even though the violence continued unabated.

Some years ago, Zbigniew Brzezinski coined the word "technetronic" to describe this new age in which communications will play a greater international role:

> The post-industrial society is becoming a "technetronic" society: a society that is shaped culturally, psychologically, socially, and economically by the impact of technology and electronics—particularly in the area of computers and communications.
>
> But while our immediate reality is being fragmented, global reality increasingly absorbs the individual, involves him, and even occasionally overwhelms him. Communications are the obvious, immediate cause. . . . The changes wrought by communications and computers make for an extraordinarily interwoven society whose members are in continuous and close audio-visual contact—constantly interacting, instantly sharing the most intense social experiences, and prompted to increased personal involvement in even the most distant problems. . . . By 1985, distance will be no excuse for delayed information from any part of the world to the powerful urban nerve centers that will mark major concentrations of the people on earth.[9]

Brzezinski's prediction has certainly come true, and the process of improved international communication is still accelerating.

Paradoxically, even with this greatly enhanced capability of involvement in world affairs, comparatively few people are well informed or even care much about what happens beyond their borders. But for those comparative few who do follow public affairs (and they are found in every nation), perceptions of the world are being formed and reshaped by this revolution in long-distance instant communications.

Our ability or lack of it to use the fruits of this technological revolution is directly related to our success or failure to act decisively and in concert as a world community. International experts worry whether the world can organize itself and deal effectively with what have been called the six major interrelated world problems: mass poverty, population, food, energy, military expenditure, and the world monetary system. Yet to organize, we must communicate, since communication is the neural system of any organization. The extent of its ability to communicate determines the boundaries of any community — be it a primitive tribe in Papua New Guinea, or a global society — and only expanded and more effective communication can make possible a viable global community.

The technology to circulate that information exists, but the barriers of illiteracy, poverty, and political constraints keep too many people in the world from receiving it. The illiteracy situation is particularly discouraging. Even though the proportion of illiterate adults declined from 44.4 to 32 percent between 1950 and 1980, the actual number increased from 700 million to 810 million, according to UNESCO. And most experts believe these figures underestimate the extent of illiteracy. The situation has been aggravated by the establishment since World War II of many new but poverty-stricken nations. UNESCO's Statistical Yearbook for 1985, listing illiteracy percentages for ninety-eight countries representing 70 percent of the world's population, counted thirty-six countries with illiteracy over 50 percent, twelve over 70 percent, and five over 80 percent.

Literacy is the key skill for modernization, education, and use of mass media. Illiteracy is widespread in Africa, so it is no wonder that there are only about 125 daily newspapers in all of Africa compared with more than 1,770 in the United States. In any country, therefore, the proportion of people able to receive news and information will vary greatly according to the availability of mass media and the the ability of people to use the media. Those living in such "information societies" as Japan or the United States are overwhelmed with information and news, while throughout the vast Third World only a tiny fraction of persons are able to participate in the international news flow.

Regardless of where they live, however, too few people take advantage of opportunities to acquire and use information in the solution of urgent transnational problems. The peoples of the dozen or so nations living on the shores of the Mediterranean Sea, for example, are confronted with accelerating pollution that is strangling that body of water. Without an unimpeded flow of information across borders to concerned leaders and experts from Greece to Algeria, corrective action to save the Mediterranean is impossible; only concerted international cooperation by all nations of the sea's borders can make an effective response possible. Fortunately, such an effort is under way.

However, whether the problem is pollution of the seas or proliferation of nuclear weapons, the fact remains that international society is marked by the absence of collective procedures, by competition rather than cooperation, and by the lack of a commitment to a common goal—in other words, a situation that approaches anarchy. The world is ruled by nation states, not by an effective international organization, and each state will usually act according to its own interests and needs.

Political scientist Robert Tucker reminds us that

> the prospects for an emergent global community cannot appear promising today. Instead of a universal conscience in the making, throughout most of the world we can observe discrete national consciences in the making. The vision of shared community that, once internalized, could prompt people to sacrifice on behalf of a common good remains at best embryonic. For the time being, the global challenges posed by nuclear weapons, grinding poverty, and burgeoning populations—to mention only the most pressing—will have to be dealt with by a world that is, in many respects as divided as ever.[10]

While the pessimistic realism of Professor Tucker cannot be denied, there is encouragement perhaps in the futuristic views of science fiction writer Arthur C. Clarke regarding the communications satellite:

What we are now doing—whether we like it or not—
indeed, whether we wish it or not—is laying the foundation of
the first global society. Whether the final planetary authority
will be an analogue of the federal systems now existing in the
United States or the USSR I do not know. I suspect that,
without any deliberate planning, such organizations as the
world meteorological and earth resources satellite system and
the world communications satellite system (of which
INTELSAT is the precursor) will eventually transcend their
individual components. At some time during the next century
they will discover, to their great surprise, that they are really
running the world.

There are many who will regard these possibilities with
alarm or distaste, and may even attempt to prevent their
fulfillment. I would remind them of the story of the wise
English king, Canute, who had his throne set upon the
seashore so he could demonstrate to his foolish courtiers that
even the king could not command the incoming tide.

The wave of the future is now rising before us. Gentlemen, do not attempt to hold it back. Wisdom lies in recognizing the inevitable—and cooperating with it. In the world that
is coming, the great powers are not great enough.[11]

Some signs of this trend are already visible; a slow but percep-
tible drift toward internationalization of the world's news media is
taking place. The world's news agencies, a few newspapers and
magazines, and some aspects of broadcasting are transcending the
national states from which they arose. Such a transition will be
welcomed by some as a contribution to better world understanding
or resented by others as efforts by some nations to impose their
models of mass communication on everyone.

The technological capability for worldwide communication
has never been greater, but then never have truly global problems
and challenges been more urgent and ominous. Too few people
anywhere understand these problems or are in a position to cooperate with others in resolving them.

Serious questions can be posed about the adequacy of today's
system of global news communication, but no doubts exist about
the importance to the world of the newspapers, news agencies, and
broadcasters that report the world's news to itself. And yet, as we
shall see, profound political and ideological differences separate

the journalists and mass communicators who staff the world's news media.

NOTES

1. Lester R. Brown, *World without Borders* (New York: Vintage Books, 1973), pp. 10–12.
2. Lester R. Brown, et al., *State of the World 1986* (New York: W. W. Norton, 1986), p. 21.
3. "India Likely to Top China Population," *Wisconsin State Journal,* April 10, 1986, p. 10.
4. Edwin Reischauer, *Toward the 21st Century: Education for a Changing World* (New York: Alfred A. Knopf, 1973), pp. 3–4.
5. American Council on Education, Higher Education Panel Reports, "General Education Requirements in the Humanities," Monograph, 1985, p. 7.
6. Harold D. Lasswell, "The Future of World Communication: Quality and Style of Life," Papers of the East-West Communication Institute, Honolulu, no. 4 (September 1972), p. 3.
7. Thomas Griffith, "Newswatch," *Time,* March 17, 1986, p. 72.
8. Walter B. Wriston, "Economic Freedom Receives a Boost," *New York Times,* April 15, 1986, p. 31. See also David Haward Bain, "Letter from Manila: How the Press Helped to Dump a Despot," *Columbia Journalism Review,* May/June 1986, pp. 27–36.
9. Zbigniew Brzezinski, *Between Two Ages: America's Role in the Technetronic Era* (New York: Viking Press, 1970), pp. 9–14.
10. Robert W. Tucker, "World Unity: A Goal Still beyond Reach," *Milwaukee Journal,* March 6, 1977, Accent section, p. 9.
11. Arthur C. Clarke, "Beyond Babel: The Century of the Communications Satellite," in *The Process and Effects of Mass Communication,* ed. W. Schramm and D. Roberts (Urbana: University of Illinois Press, 1971), p. 963.

2
Clashing Ideologies:
Five Concepts
of the
Press

A journalist is a grumbler, a censurer, a giver of advice, a regent of sovereigns, a tutor of nations. Four hostile newspapers are more to be feared than a thousand bayonets.

— *Napoleon Bonaparte*

Abuses of the freedom of speech ought to be repressed, but to whom dare we commit the power of doing it?

— *Benjamin Franklin*

DESPITE the impressive technological improvements in international news exchanges, editors and broadcasters have no control over how the reports of the events of the day emerge from the global news prism, whose planes and surfaces have been hewn and polished by diverse and frequently antagonistic political and social systems. As the news passes through the prism, what one journalist considers to be truthful, objective reporting can bend into what another journalist elsewhere in the world considers to be distortion or propaganda.

For despite our impressive technological expertise, political differences and cultural conflicts prevent the international news process from working smoothly and harmoniously. More and faster news communication across national borders does not automatically lead to better understanding; often it results in enmity and distrust, since the profound cultural and social differences that characterize the world community preclude agreement on what is legitimate news. One person's truth is another's propaganda.

As a result, international journalism in recent years has been the subject of increasing rancor and mutual hostility and suspicion. Mass communication's powerful ability to publicize, to expose, to glorify, to criticize, to denigrate, and to mislead or propagandize is universally recognized and often feared. At one time or another, government officials in every land become unhappy or dismayed with the press and often do something about it. In the West, a president or prime minister may complain bitterly that his or her programs are unfairly reported by press opponents. In an African country, an offending Associated Press correspondent may be thrown into jail and personally beaten by the nation's dictator, as actually happened in the former Central African Empire. And throughout the world, journalists have become the victims of violence from those who don't want particular events reported.

The differing perceptions about the nature and role of journalism and mass communication are rooted in divergent political systems and historical traditions and are reflected in five political concepts of the press found in the world today: (1) Authoritarian, (2) Western, (3) Communist, (4) Revolutionary, and (5) Developmental (or Third World).[1] These are normative concepts that reflect how the media ideally should perform under certain conditions and values. Yet, an analysis of these contrasting approaches to the role and function of transnational journalism can help us understand some of the issues that divide the world's press.

Authoritarianism is the oldest and most pervasive concept and has spawned two twentieth-century modifications: the Communist and Developmental concepts. The Western concept, under which the press in Western democracies generally functions, represents a fundamental alternative to the Authoritarian concept and contains elements of both eighteenth-century libertarianism and twentieth-century views of social responsibility. The Revolutionary concept has one trait in common with the Western: they both try to operate outside of government controls. The Developmental concept is an emerging pattern associated with the new nations of the Third World, most of them lacking adequate media resources.

Newspapers, television, and other mass media, always and everywhere, function within some kinds of governmental, societal, and economic constraints. Even the "freest" or most independent press system must deal with varying degrees of regulation by political authority. In the relationship between government and mass communication, the basic question is not whether government controls the press but the nature and extent of those controls. For all press systems exist somewhere along a continuum from complete control (absolute authoritarianism) at one end to no controls (pure libertarianism) at the other. Absolute freedom of expression is a myth. Beyond that, controls on the press are so varied and complex that it is difficult, if not impossible, to compare press freedom in one nation with that in another. In one country, newspapers may be under harsh, arbitrary political restraints; in another they may be under more subtle yet real economic and corporate restrictions.

A basic tenet of the following analysis is that all press systems reflect the values of the political and economic systems of the nations within which they operate. The trend toward internationalization notwithstanding, print and broadcast systems are still controlled and regulated by their own national governments. And in this era of transnational communication, journalists from an open society often must work and collect news in a closed or autocratic society, thereby increasing opportunities for friction between divergent concepts.

Authoritarian Concept

Authoritarianism was in effect at the time the printing press was invented by Gutenburg in the midfifteenth century, and in the years since, more people have lived under an authoritarian press than under any other. The basic principle of authoritarianism is quite simple: the press is always subject to the direct or implied control of the state or sovereign. A printing press or a broadcasting facility cannot be used to challenge, criticize, or in any way undermine the ruler. The press functions from the top down; the king or ruler decides what shall be published because truth (and information) is essentially a monopoly of those in authority.

There is much in Western political philosophy, developed over many centuries, that stresses the central importance of authority in political theory. From Plato's *Republic* through Hobbes's *Leviathan* to Hegel and Marx, the all-powerful state is given both the right and duty to sustain and protect itself in any way necessary for its survival.

To the authoritarian, diversity of views is wasteful and irresponsible, dissent an annoying nuisance and often subversive, and consensus and standardization are logical and sensible goals for mass communication. There is a certain compelling logic behind this.

As the eighteenth-century Englishman, Dr. Samuel Johnson, wrote:

> Every society has a right to preserve public peace and order, and therefore has a good right to prohibit the propagation of opinions which have a dangerous tendency. To say the magistrate has this right is using an inadequate word: it is the society for which the magistrate is the agent. He may be morally and theologically wrong in restraining the propagation of opinions which he thinks dangerous but he is politically right.[2]

To many in authority around the world today, these views are not unreasonable, certainly not to leaders of poverty-stricken developing nations faced with monumental tasks of political integration and economic development. Why, under such circumstances, should government tolerate what it considers disruptive and seditious views? Why should it permit foreign journalists to enter its country and then write critical and negative reports to the outside world, undermining the authority and prestige of the ruling government?

Under traditional authoritarianism, the press operates outside of government and is permitted to gather and publish news, but it must function for the "good of the state." The government usually leaves the press alone as long as it does not criticize authority or challenge the leadership in any way. If the press does attack government, then the political authority intervenes, imposing censorship or even closing down publications and jailing editors. Under the Authoritarian concept, the constraint of potential censorship, if not actual prior restraint itself, always exists. Editors and reporters exercise a good deal of self-censorship, but never know for sure just how far they can go without triggering official disfavor and intervention. They must support the status quo and not advocate change, criticize the nation's leadership, or give offense to dominant moral or political values.

So wherever governments arbitrarily intervene and suppress independent newspapers and broadcasters, there the Authoritarian concept flourishes. The media situation in right-wing military regimes such as those of General Augusto Pinochet in Chile or the junta in Argentina during the late 1970s — when thousands of Argentine citizens, including journalists, disappeared — illustrates the concept in action.

A specific, well-publicized example would be the incident in Indonesia in April 1986 as President Ronald Reagan arrived on an official visit accompanied by a planeload of Western journalists. Moments before he was to be greeted on Bali by President Suharto, two Australian broadcast journalists were pulled off the press plane and ordered out of the country. This action was in retaliation for an unflattering article in the *Sydney Morning Herald* charging corruption and cronyism in Suharto's government. In addition, a *New York Times* correspondent based in Thailand, Barbara Crossette, was also barred from covering the Reagan visit, presumably because of unhappiness over her reporting.[3]

Authoritarianism is widespread today, especially if, as some scholars aver, the Communist and Developmental concepts are understood to be variations of traditional authoritarianism.

However, authoritarian practices cannot always be clearly delimited. Democracies in time of war or crisis (Britain during World War II, for example) sometimes adopt authoritarian controls on the press. And democratic France, under Charles DeGaulle and several of his successors, suffered under heavy-handed authoritarian control of its television system. In many nations, especially in Latin America, the media have moved back and forth between freedom and controls as the governments changed from military to democratic regimes.

Foreign correspondents pose a special challenge to authoritarian regimes, and Western journalists often encounter a variety of difficulties: entry visas are denied; stories are censored; telex and comsat facilities are refused; and sometimes reporters are harassed, mistreated, jailed, or expelled.

Western Concept

The Western concept represents a distinct deviation from the traditional authoritarian controls and evolved during the rise of democracies in Europe and North America. For example, during the long constitutional struggle in Britain between the crown, the courts, and the Commons and later, in the United States, a press relatively free of arbitrary government controls slowly evolved.

In fact, one definition of freedom of the press is the right of the press to report, comment on, and criticize its own government without retaliation or threat of retaliation from that government. This has been called the "right to talk politics." Historically, seditious libel meant criticism of government, laws, or officials. The absence of seditious libel as a crime has been regarded as the true pragmatic test of a country's freedom of expression, since politically relevant speech is what press freedom is mostly about.

By this demanding test — the right to talk politics — the Western concept is comparatively rare in today's world, although many authoritarian governments give it lip service. A free or independent press is usually found in only a dozen or more Western nations that share these characteristics: (1) a system of law that provides meaningful protection to individual civil liberties and property rights (here common law nations such as the United States and Britain seem to do better than nations such as France or Italy, with civil law traditions); (2) high average levels of per capita income, education, and literacy; (3) governance by constitutional parliamentary democracy or at least with legitimate political oppositions; (4) sufficient capital or private enterprise to support media of news communication; and (5) an established tradition of independent journalism.

Any list of nations meeting these criteria for a Western press today would certainly include the United States, the United Kingdom, Canada, Sweden, West Germany, France, the Netherlands, Belgium, Australia, New Zealand, Norway, Denmark, Austria, Iceland, Ireland, Israel, Italy, and Switzerland. In addition to these Western nations, highly developed and westernized Japan surely should be added. And India, the world's most populous democracy, has enjoyed a remarkably free press despite its diverse problems.

Journalists in many other nations support and practice the Western concept, but because of political instability, their media over the years have swung back and forth between freedom and control. Such nations include Spain, Greece, Portugal, Colombia, Sri Lanka, Brazil, Argentina, Chile, Turkey, and Venezuela.

By and large, the Western nations that meet the criteria include the handful that do most of the world's news gathering from other nations and whose correspondents most often come in conflict with authoritarian regimes. For the Western concept holds most strongly that a government — any government, here or abroad — should not interfere in the process of collecting and disseminating news. The press, in theory, must be independent of authority and, of course, exist outside of government and be well protected by law and custom from arbitrary government interference. Not many journalists in the world work under such conditions.

The ideals of Western libertarian journalism are, to a large extent, a by-product of the Enlightenment and the liberal political tradition reflected in the writings of John Milton, John Locke, Thomas Jefferson, and John Stuart Mill. Primarily, there must be a diversity of views and news sources available — a "marketplace of ideas" from which the public can choose what it wishes to read and believe. For no one or no authority, spiritual or temporal, has a monopoly on truth. U.S. Judge Learned Hand said it best:

> That [newspaper] industry serves one of the most vital of all general interests: the dissemination of news from as many different sources, and with as many different facets as is possible. . . . It presupposes that right conclusions are more likely to be gathered out of a multitude of tongues than through any kind of authoritarian selection. To many this is, and always will be, folly; but we have staked upon it our all.[4]

Underlying this diversity of views is the faith that citizens will somehow make the right choices about what to believe if enough voices are heard and government keeps its hands off.

In American political theory, this libertarian view is based upon certain values deemed inherent in a free press: (1) by gathering public information and scrutinizing government, self-government and democracy become possible; (2) an unfettered press assures that a diversity of views and news will be read and heard; (3)

a system of free expression provides autonomy for individuals to lead free and productive lives; and (4) it enables an independent press to serve as a check on abuses of power by government.[5]

Carried over to the international context, the Western concept argues that there must be a free flow of information unimpeded by any intervention by any nation. No government anywhere should obstruct the gathering and dissemination of legitimate news. Only news media free of official restraints, it is argued, will be credible to readers and viewers here and abroad.

Advocates say the Western concept serves the cause of global news flow in several important ways. First, it makes possible the gathering and dissemination of reliable and accurate news. Then, it provides news and important information to peoples living in authoritarian regimes that censor their own media. International shortwave radio broadcasters—BBC World Service, Voice of America, Deutsche Welle, Radio Free Europe, and others—relay news from Western news gatherers. During upheavals, people in non-Western nations often turn to shortwave radio to learn what is happening in their own country (see Chap. 6, Polishing the Prism: Public Diplomacy and Propaganda).

Furthermore, by serving as a "surrogate press" for peoples denied access to news, the Western media contribute to the promotion of human rights by publicizing the fate of political prisoners, including imprisoned journalists. Amnesty International has lauded this role of the international press in publicizing human rights violations, whether in Argentina, the Soviet Union, Chile, Uganda, Turkey, or elsewhere and believes that a political prisoner is more likely to be released if his or her imprisonment is known to the outside world. Sometimes that news comes from Third World journalists courageous enough to defy their own authoritarian governments.

This is not to say that Western news media are without shortcomings—serious ones—or that people in Western democracies have unlimited freedom to criticize their governments. Political freedom does not preclude economic and corporate interference with journalistic practices. A privately owned media system will, in varying degrees, reflect the interests and concerns of its owners. Yet to stay independent of outside controls, including government, the media must be financially strong and profitable. Journalistic excellence and profitability are not identical goals, although some of the best news media are also very profitable; for some owners, however, making money is the primary purpose of journalism, and independence and public service mean little.

Furthermore, diversity at both national and international levels appears to be in decline, and the marked increase of media conglomerates and ownership concentration has reduced the number of independent voices heard in the marketplace. More and more newspapers, magazines, and broadcasting stations are becoming submerged into huge media organizations.[6] In some democracies, such as Norway and Sweden, the government maintains diversity of political views by providing subsidies to the newspapers of the various political parties, a practice not without a potential danger to press independence.

Some modifications of the Western concept fall under the rubric of Social Responsibility. This view holds that the media have clear obligations of public service that transcend moneymaking. Public service implies professional standards for journalists as well as for reliable and objective reporting. The media are obligated, in addition, to ensure that all voices and views in the community are heard. Further, government is granted a limited role in intervening in media operations and in regulating conditions if public interests are not being adequately served. Government regulation of broadcasting in the United States, for example, offers a good example of the Social Responsibility position.

Two other related modifications of the Western concept are the Democratic Socialist and the Democratic Participant. Expressing fears of the abuses of private ownership, the Democratic Socialist says state action is needed to institute new forms of ownership and management and to intervene in the economics of the media.[7]

Similarly, Democratic Participant theory reflects a reaction against commercialization and monopolization of the privately owned media as well as against the centralism and bureaucratization of public broadcasting. Denis McQuail summarizes several of its principles: (1) media should exist primarily for their audiences and not for media organizations, professionals, or clients of media; (2) individual citizens and minority groups have rights of access to media (rights to communicate) and rights to be served by media according to the peoples' own determination of need; (3) organization and content of the media should not be subject to centralized political or state bureaucratic control; and finally, (4) small-scale, interactive, and participative media forms are better than large-scale, professionalized media.[8]

These evolving views, which represent some disillusionment with mass media performance, are found throughout Western democracies but especially in Northern Europe. The major disadvantage of these attitudes is that such decentralized, small-scale media are less able to check the abuses of government power whether at home or abroad.

Communist Concept

In some places in the world, the Western concept is regarded as a culture-bound by-product of industrialized capitalist nations and as such is irrelevant to the needs and problems of Socialist and developing nations. Furthermore, some consider it fallacious to judge the press of non-Western nations by Western standards.

Lenin maintained that a nation's press always served the dominant (ruling) class in any society; therefore, he concluded, access to the press must be denied to certain unsupportive elements of society. Furthermore, freedom of the press, in his view, consisted not so much in the right to say what one wished, but in controlling the economic structure of the press—in short, newsprint, printing equipment, and buildings.

As the leader most responsible for articulating the Communist concept, Lenin once wrote:

> Capitalists call "freedom of the press" that state of affairs when censorship is removed and all parties are free to publish any newspapers. In this very thing there is no freedom of the press but freedom to deceive the oppressed and exploited mass by the rich, the bourgeoisie. "Freedom of the press" of a bourgeois society consists in freedom of the rich systematically, unceasingly, and daily in the millions of copies to deceive, corrupt, and fool the exploited and oppressed mass of the people, the poor.[9]

In the Communist view, a free and independent press becomes a divisive, costly luxury that does not serve the needs of the state and hence the people. Mass media controlled and directed by the

Communist party can concentrate on the serious task of nation building by publishing news relating to the entire society's policies and goals as determined by the top party leadership. Lenin saw the press's first function to be as an organizing instrument to inform and control a revolutionary party apparatus seeking to overthrow a government. To him the press was an integral part of the Communist party, which was itself seen as a teacher to instruct the masses and lead the proletariat.

The press and broadcasting are perceived as instruments, along with other institutions such as schools and labor organizations, with which to rule. In a well-known phrase, the press is "agitator, propagandist, and organizer." Media serve as implements of revelation (by revealing ideology along with the purposes and policies of party leaders) as well as instruments of unity and consensus.

Essentially, the Communist concept differs from the traditional authoritarian view in that the communication media are state owned, not privately owned, and serve a positive function of helping the government to rule. The press is required to do something, not merely avoid offending the rulers. In the Soviet Union and in other nations of the Communist commonwealth, such as the German Democratic Republic, Poland, Hungary, China, Bulgaria, Czechoslovakia, and Rumania, the press is integrated into the monolithic Communist state. Whereas the Western libertarian views press freedom as freedom *from* government, the Communist concept regards it as freedom *within* the all-powerful state to pursue the goals of the state.

It is ironic that although the Soviet press was conceived in theory and matured in practice as a subversive and revolutionary instrument before the 1917 Revolution, it reached full maturity under Stalin and has since become in postwar Eastern Europe an instrument of conformity and consensus while still espousing Lenin's revolutionary ideology. The elaborate media systems of the Soviet Union and its Socialist neighbors have become, in practice, conservative caretakers of the status quo, staunch supporters of long-standing Communist regimes.

In the Soviet Union today, political power rests with the party, the police, and the press. The main function of the press is to promote the policies of leadership and to help control the society. News is quite secondary. As a result, the press is often boring and predictable, and stories about abuses of power, corruption, and official incompetence are usually not reported. As one expert on the Soviet press has said, "The Leninist mission of the Soviet press is to shape public opinion at home and to influence — or confuse — it abroad. The Soviet leadership dislikes undertaking any dangerous or controversial action without first having prepared public opinion."[10] Elaborate media campaigns preceded such Soviet actions as the 1968 invasion of Czechoslovakia and the boycott of the 1984 Olympics in Los Angeles.

No attention is given in the Soviet media to the views of dissidents or advocates of radical or revolutionary change. The efforts of Western journalists to report the views of Soviet dissidents, a good news story by Western standards, are much resented and often thwarted by Soviet authorities who consider such news-gathering efforts serious interference in their internal affairs. As Lenin said, there is no freedom for enemies of the state.

Implicit in the Communist concept is the conviction that the Communist party must maintain a monopoly on all mass communication. There must be no privately owned media. Communist regimes have never been particularly hospitable to Western journalists. During the Stalin years, the few foreign reporters admitted faced censorship, visa problems, and restricted access and travel. Few Western publications were permitted through the Iron Curtain, and radio broadcasts to Eastern Europe were jammed. In recent years, the Communist regimes have worked out a modus vivendi of sorts with Western reporters, and things are more open than before. The gathering of news in Communist societies, however, remains difficult and demanding; Western journalists are still harassed on occasion.

Since the death of Mao Zedong, the People's Republic of China (that other great Communist nation) has become more accessible to foreign reporters. Bureaus were opened in 1979 in Beijing by AP and UPI as well as the *New York Times, Washington Post, Los Angeles Times,* and *Wall Street Journal.* The reforms in Chinese society undertaken by Deng Xiaoping have brought such marked changes in the media as increased use of advertising, more entertainment features, and Western-style news stories. However, the basic function of mass communication in China remains the same — to support the policies and goals of the party leadership.

Part of the difficulty in reporting Communist societies to the

West stems from their definition of news. Under the Communist concept, news is information that serves the interests of the state, that advances its goals and policies. Information of interest and importance to a large number of people is not necessarily news, especially if in some way it embarrasses the political leadership.

A major example of Soviet response to bad news at home was the handling of the nuclear accident at the Chernobyl power station in April 1986. To the outside world, the extraordinary effort of the Soviet government to restrict information about the disaster was almost as striking as the fact that radiation was spewed into the air, reaching to Scandinavia and Eastern Europe. Observers called it a reflexive retreat into secrecy that seemed to show the Kremlin unwilling to concede the smallest failing before its people and the world.

Only after Sweden detected steep increases in radioactivity two days after the accident and demanded information did the Soviet government issue the first brief statement of forty-four words, barely acknowledging that an accident had occurred.[11]

Instead of supplying crucial information promptly about the nature of the accident itself or about the kinds and amounts of radiation being released, the Soviet media accused the press of the West of exaggerating the disaster to "whip up anti-Soviet hysteria." At the same time, TASS news agency released a letter from Mikhail Gorbachev criticizing continued American nuclear testing.[12]

Soviet handling of the Chernobyl event proved a public relations disaster for the Kremlin. Throughout Europe, harsh criticism was directed at the Soviet Union for failing to provide full and prompt information about the radioactivity spreading over Europe and for not even warning its own citizens in the affected areas. Soviet efforts to minimize the story in the first days were contradicted by photos from military and civilian satellites that graphically showed details of the disaster. Gradually, the Soviet media did report details in bits and pieces. The fact that 92,000 people had been evacuated was tucked away in an *Izvestia* article about two weeks after the fact.

In Communist nations, aircraft crashes or other domestic disasters are not reported quickly and fully, as they are in the West. In July 1976, for example, the Chinese government saw no particular reason to inform the outside world of a major earthquake in Tangshan, so only unconfirmed rumors filtered through to the outside world. Not until early 1977 did the story come out and the outside world learn that rescue workers had estimated about 750,000 people were killed or injured in what was perhaps the worst natural disaster of the twentieth century. (The Chinese government itself did not officially acknowledge the loss of life until November 22, 1979, when a small item appeared in the Communist party paper, the *People's Daily*, admitting to 242,000 killed and 164,000 injured.) Clearly, despite the pervasive international news system, major events can still go unreported in countries living with the Communist concept, though with communications satellites it is becoming more difficult to conceal the event itself.

In addition to TASS, which has personnel in ninety-four countries and exchange agreements with forty news agencies, *Pravda, Izvestia,* and Novosti (the feature news agency) maintain correspondents abroad. But the Soviet foreign correspondent is essentially an emissary of the Soviet Union and tends to stress official views in reporting from other lands. News gathering is more akin to intelligence gathering: sending back information of use and interest to officialdom rather than to the average reader. Much of the news gathered abroad does not reach the average Soviet citizen. Soviet journalists carry diplomatic passports and are sometimes implicated in espionage activities and, on occasion, are expelled along with other Soviet diplomats when such activities are exposed.

The Soviet media are integrated, planned, and used in a way that the older authoritarian press almost never was. Under traditional authoritarianism, the media were merely controlled; the Soviet media serve the state just as the navy and railroads do.

Revolutionary Concept

Lenin himself provided some of the ideology and the rationale for another and more ephemeral view, the Revolutionary. Simply stated, this is a concept of illegal and subversive communication utilizing the press and broadcasting to overthrow a government or wrest control from alien or otherwise rejected rulers.

Lenin in his famous work, "What Is to be Done?" (written in exile before the 1917 Revolution), proposed that the revolutionaries establish a nationwide legal newspaper inside czarist Russia.

Such a paper could obviously not advocate revolutionary goals, but its distribution system could be an excellent mechanism for a political machine. The newspaper, Lenin postulated, would be a cover for a farflung revolutionary organization and a means of communication between followers, a way to keep them in touch.

The early *Pravda,* although it was not a legal paper (and was edited by Stalin at one time), was published outside czarist Russia, and smuggled copies were widely distributed—a fine example of the Revolutionary concept.

The revolutionary press is a press of people who believe strongly that the government they live under does not serve their interests and should be overthrown. They owe such a government no loyalty. Pure examples are difficult to find, but one surely was the underground press in Nazi-occupied France during World War II. The editors and journalists of the *Editions Minuit* literally risked their lives to put out their papers and pamphlets. Many other publications called "underground newspapers," such as those that flourished in America during the antiwar protests in the late 1960s, were not truly revolutionary because they were generally tolerated by authorities and the risks of publishing were not great; some editors were harassed by local authorities, but none faced firing squads.

Better contemporary examples of the Revolutionary concept are the *samizdat* ("self-publishing" in Russian), the clandestinely typed and mimeographed copies of books, political tracts, and the like, that are passed at great risk from hand to hand among dissidents inside the Soviet Union. Often such publications are merely expressing grievances or petitioning for civil rights, but to authoritarian regimes such expression is clearly revolutionary and subversive.

The history of anticolonialist movements in the Third World is replete with examples of the Revolutionary press concept. Throughout the British Empire, especially in West Africa, political dissidents published small newspapers, often handwritten, that first expressed grievances against the British rulers, then encouraged nationalism, and finally advocated political independence. Aspiring political leaders such as Azikiwe, Awolowo, Nkrumah, Kaunda, and Kenyatta were editors of these small political papers that informed and helped organize the budding political parties and nationalist movements.[13] British authorities were surprisingly tolerant, even though they disapproved of and sometimes acted against the publications and their editors.

Much in the Anglo-American tradition supported these papers, and the editors claimed the rights of British journalists. Had not Thomas Paine used political pamphlets to help run the British out of the American Colonies? Had not Thomas Jefferson (and his words were echoed later by Supreme Court Justice William O. Douglas) said the people have a right to revolution, including the right to subsequent revolutions if that proved necessary?

In the postindependence years, radio broadcasting has become a valuable tool of revolutionary groups seeking to overthrow the fragile governments of the Third World. Black Africa has been plagued with numerous coups d'etat, and during times of acute political crisis, radio broadcasting has often played a significant role as the primary medium of mass communication in most nations. Rebels have recognized the importance of controlling information at the political center of power. Hence, insurgents often seize the radio station before heading for the presidential palace. Military struggles during a coup attempt often occur outside the broadcast station, because if rebels can announce over the nation's only radio station that a coup has been accomplished (even while the issue is still in doubt), it helps accomplish the desired end.[14]

More recently, two other communication devices—the Xerox machine and the audio cassette—have proved quite useful in revolutionary efforts. In Iran, the revolution of the Ayatollah Khomeini has been called the first cassette revolution. Thousands of cassette recordings of the Ayatollah's speeches propagating his revolutionary ideas were played in the mosques, which were not kept under surveillance by the Shah's secret police. These small, portable instruments were able to reach millions while circumventing the government-controlled press, radio, and television. At the same time, when revolutionary "night letters" and pamphlets arrived mysteriously at offices in Tehran, sympathetic secretaries made many photocopies, quickly and more secretly than possible with a printing press.

Anthony Sampson says that "the period of television and radio monopolies may prove a passing phase, as we find ourselves in a much more open field of communications, with cassettes and copied documents taking the place of the books and pamphlets that undermined 18th century governments." He suggested an epitaph for the Shah's regime: "He forgot the cassette."[15]

Even though television and radio stations—more controllable than the printing press—can give autocratic governments a monopoly of news and propaganda, the Revolutionary concept still can be fostered in divided societies by innovations in more personal and decentralized communication methods. The video cassette recorder (VCR), despite its cost, is spreading rapidly in societies with controlled media systems, from Saudi Arabia to the Soviet Union, because it enables individual viewers to select their own television programs and not be passive recipients of officially sanctioned programs. This has created a worldwide market for smuggled video cassettes, usually of movies and popular music from the West.

Developmental Concept

By its very nature, the Revolutionary concept is a short-term affair; the successful subversive use of mass communication to topple a despised regime is self-limiting. Once goals are achieved, the gains must be consolidated, and then another concept takes over. But in recent decades, a variation of the Authoritarian—the Developmental concept—has been emerging in the wake of political independence in impoverished nations throughout the Third World.

The Developmental concept is an amorphous and curious mixture of ideas, rhetoric, influences, and grievances. As yet, the concept is not clearly defined. There are aspects straight out of Lenin and the Communist concept of the press. Perhaps of greater importance are the influences of Western social scientists who have posited a major role for mass communication in the process of nation building in newly independent countries. American academics such Wilbur Schramm, Daniel Lerner, and others, all libertarians at heart, have argued that the communication process is central to the achievement of national integration and economic development; in doing so they may have unintentionally provided a rationale for autocratic press controls.

Other more radical academics such as Dallas Smythe of Canada, Kaarle Nordenstreng of Finland, and Herbert Schiller of the United States have echoed Marxist views and added a strong touch of anti-Americanism to the concept. For the concept is to some extent a critique of and reaction against the West and its transnational media. It also reflects the frustrations and anger of poor and media-deficient nations of the Third World.

A major international agency, the United Nations Educational, Scientific and Cultural Organization (UNESCO), has provided a forum and sounding board for the expression of the Developmental concept, which is an approach to mass communication of nations that are clearly lacking in newspapers and broadcasting facilities—the world's "have-nots" in media resources.

Generally, the concept holds that:

• All the instruments of mass communication—newspapers, radio, television, motion pictures, national news services—must be mobilized by the central government to aid in the great tasks of nation building: fighting illiteracy and poverty, building a political consciousness, assisting in economic development. Implicit here is the Social Responsibility view that the government must step in and provide adequate media service when the private sector is unable to do so, as is the case in many poor nations.

• The media therefore should support authority, not challenge it. Dissent and criticism have no place, in part because the alternative to the ruling government would be chaos, it is argued. Freedom of the press, then, can be restricted according to the development needs of the society.

• Information (or truth) thus becomes the property of the state; the flow of power (and truth) between the governors and the governed works from the top down, as in traditional authoritarianism. Information or news is a scarce national resource; it must be utilized to further the national goals.

• Implied but not often articulated is the view that individual rights of expression and other civil liberties are somewhat irrelevant in the face of the overwhelming problems of poverty, disease, illiteracy, and ethnicity that face a majority of these nations. (Critics argue that the concept provides a palatable rationale for old-fashioned authoritarianism.)

• This concept of a guided press further implies that in international news, each nation has a sovereign right to control foreign journalists and the flow of news back and forth across its borders.

Some critics say that central to the Developmental concept is the rejection of the Western view. As British journalist Rosemary Righter argues, there is a growing feeling that the Western model of the press is undesirable in itself. Instead of backing diversity and free flow, the mass media must adopt a didactic, even ideological, role of explaining to the people their part in forging a new social order.[16]

In fact, one of the catch phrases of the concept is that the world needs a "New World Information Order" to redress these imbalances.

Western news media are attacked on several scores. To begin with, some critics say the Western international media are too monopolistic and powerful; they penetrate too widely and effectively. The world news agencies — Associated Press, United Press International, Reuters, and Agence France Presse — are particular targets, charged with creating a clear imbalance, a one-way flow, in the dissemination of information, which favors the affluent North.

Furthermore, Western media represent an alien viewpoint, which they impose on nations trying to build independent modern identities. Traditional cultures, it is charged, have been threatened by the inundation of news and mass culture — television programs, pop music, movies, video and audio cassettes — principally from America and Britain. Such domination, it is argued, amounts to cultural aggression. Western media, these critics insist, lack both the accuracy and objectivity on which they have based their claims for preeminence.

Finally, a few proponents of the Developmental concept charge that the Western media are part of an international conspiracy by which the economic and political interests of the capitalist nations are using global mass communication to dominate, even subjugate, the Third World.

The Developmental concept is a view of mass communication from the many nations of the Third World where most people are colored, poor, ill-nourished, and illiterate, and it reflects resentments against the West where people are mainly Caucasians (except in Japan), affluent, and literate. The concept is directly related to what some feel is the major problem facing the world today: the widening gap between the rich and the poor, debt-ridden nations. The same nations that decry the trade and GNP imbalances between North and South also excoriate the Western news media.

Righter, of the *Sunday Times,* believes there is an organized campaign under way—through supranational agencies like UNESCO, in intergovernment groupings, and in a number of academic and quasi-political institutions—to give the concept of a guided press international respectability.[17]

In the continuing frictions between the Western and Developmental concepts several qualifications are in order. Third World advocacy of a guided media system comes mainly from political leaders and government representatives. Some journalists support this, but many others throughout the Third World—in India, Nigeria, the Philippines, Kenya, Pakistan, and other countries—advocate and try to practice, often under great difficulty, journalism that is independent of state control.

Some perceive the Developmental concept as only a temporary and transitional condition pending achievement of a more developed and participant society. In numerous countries where government-controlled media are advocated by unelected leaders and their representatives in UNESCO, there are journalists, lawyers, and academics who support the values of independent journalism and the free flow of information. And, curiously, government officials in many countries with government-controlled media insist their newspapers and broadcasting are much freer and open than they actually are.

The controversy engendered by these conflicting concepts of mass communication—between the Western and the Developmental, with its strong overtones of authoritarianism—has been marked by rancor in recent years but has shown some signs of abating. There are valid arguments on both sides of this political and ideological confrontation, each reflecting differing social, political, and cultural traditions that are difficult to reconcile. As the world becomes more interdependent, the conflicts over how news and information are to be controlled become ever-more serious and abrasive.

Although few if any nations fit neatly into these five normative concepts of the press, the concepts may still be useful in illustrating some of the divergent perceptions of the nature of news and how it should be disseminated. But the problems surrounding the gathering and delivery of international news are more complex and varied than can be neatly categorized to fit into set classifications.

And, despite the variety of news and views refracted through the world news prism, the great bulk of foreign news is gathered and disseminated by Western news media.

NOTES

1. For this analysis, the author owes a debt to that influential book by Fred Siebert, Theodore Peterson, and Wilbur Schramm, *Four Theories of the Press* (Urbana: University of Illinois Press, 1956). For purposes of this transnational comparison of press systems, the Libertarian and Social Responsibility theories are both included within the Western concept.
2. Ibid., p. 36.
3. Gerald Boyd, "Indonesia Bars Two Journalists in Reagan Party," *New York Times,* April 30, 1986, p. 1.
4. Associated Press v. United States, 52 F. Supp. 362, 372 (1943).
5. See Vincent Blasi, "The Checking Value in First Amendment Theory," *American Bar Foundation Research Journal,* 1977, no. 3 (Summer):521–649.
6. Ben H. Bagdikian, "The U.S. Media: Supermarket or Assembly Line," *Journal of Communication* 35, no. 3 (Summer 1985):97–109.
7. Robert Picard, "Revisions of the 'Four Theories of the Press,' " *Mass Communication Review,* Winter/Spring 1982–83, p. 27.
8. Denis McQuail, *Mass Communication Theory: An Introduction* (Beverly Hills: Sage, 1983), pp. 96–97.
9. Ithiel de Sola Pool, "The Mass Media and Politics in the Modernization Process," in *Communications and Political Development,* ed. Lucian Pye (Princeton, N. J.: Princeton University Press, 1963), pp. 230ff.
10. Raymond H. Anderson, "USSR: How Lenin's Guidelines Shape the News," *Columbia Journalism Review,* September/October 1984, p. 40.
11. Serge Schmemann, "The Soviet Secrecy," *New York Times,* May 1, 1986, p. 1.
12. Philip Taubman, "Soviet Keeps Lid on News Coverage," *New York Times,* April 30, 1986, p. 7.
13. E. Lloyd Murphy, "Nationalism and the Press in British West Africa" (Master's thesis, University of Wisconsin-Madison, 1967).
14. William Hachten, "Broadcasting and Political Crisis," in *Broadcasting in Africa: A Continental Survey of Radio and Television,* ed. Sydney Head (Philadelphia: Temple University Press, 1974), pp. 395–98.
15. Anthony Sampson, "Rebel Poli-Techs," *New York Times,* May 6, 1979, opposite editorial page.
16. Rosemary Righter, *Whose News? Politics, the Press and the Third World* (New York: Times Books, 1979), pp. 14–15.
17. Ibid., p. 21.

3

International News System

> What we are building now is the nervous system of mankind, which will link together the whole human race, for better or worse, in a unity which no earlier age could have imagined.
>
> —*Arthur C. Clarke*

IN October 1985, it happened again. American hostages were seized by Middle East terrorists and the world once more held its breath—and watched its television sets. This time it was not an airliner but the Italian cruise ship, the *Achille Lauro,* whose passenger list included four Palestinian gunmen who took over the luxury liner in Egyptian waters near Port Said. Immediately, the world's news media zeroed in on the story. Television, radio, and newspapers reported each breaking development through to the dramatic ending four days later when U.S. Navy jets forced an Egyptian airliner carrying the hijackers to land at a Sicilian airfield.

Reports on every aspect of the *Achille Lauro* story flooded newsrooms and broadcast stations around the world. But this story, like most major news stories, was essentially reported by journalists working for the great news organizations of a handful of Western nations. For Americans, Western Europeans, Japanese, and some others, news—like electricity, water, and gas—has become an essential service that is taken for granted. By merely turning on a radio or television set or picking up a newspaper at the door, we expect to find the latest news, whether it be from the Middle East, Europe, Africa, or outer space.

Indeed, it is hard to remember when breaking news was not available immediately (like any other public utility) at the flick of a switch; the technicalities of its delivery are of little public concern and at best only dimly understood. The fact is, however, that global news communication is of fairly recent origin. The far-flung apparatus or "system" through which news flows around the world has evolved and developed mainly since World War II along with our modern technetronic society. We learned, for example, of the important events of World War II many hours or even several days *after* the events — and then through radio or newspapers; just thirty years later, the day's clashes in Vietnam were brought to us in full color on our home television screens at dinnertime. It goes without saying that the public's perceptions of wars have always been colored by the way journalists have reported them, but television pictures of Vietnam had an unusually strong impact on public attitudes. And today, as with the *Achille Lauro* incident, the public follows many dramatic news events *while* they are taking place.

In this century, and particularly since 1945, an intricate web of international communications has been spun about the planet, greatly expanding the capability for news and political interaction at a time when the need for information has become so much more urgent. This rapid growth of what Colin Cherry has termed an "explosion" in mass communication around the world has had widespread significance — for world journalism, for the flow of news and information, for the cultural impact of motion pictures and television from the West (which some critics call "cultural imperialism"), and for the institutions of international communication: news agencies, broadcast networks, and international newspapers, magazines, and other publications. And today, the world reacts politically much more quickly to events than ever before.

As we become an ever-more interdependent world community with common problems, if not common goals, the world's ability to communicate effectively to all its parts has been greatly expanded.

As Cherry described it, this communication explosion has three aspects: *geographically,* vast areas of the world (Africa, South Asia, Latin America) have been drawn into the global communication network for the first time; the *amount* of traffic and the *number* of messages carried in the system have multiplied geometrically; and the *technical complexity* of both the new hardware and the skills and specialized knowledge to maintain and run the network have become increasingly sophisticated.

"For two thousand years and more the means of distant communications were various postal services, derived from the Roman *cursus publicus,* working at the speed of the horse; and then the explosion hit us, not immediately upon the invention of the telegraph, but nearly a century later," Cherry wrote. "It is the sheer suddenness of the explosion which is of such profound social importance, principally following the Second World War."[1]

From crystal sets in 1920 to a television service in 1937, Cherry pointed out, was only seventeen years. The first transistor appeared in 1948, the first *Sputnik* followed only nine years later, and electronic memory chips, the silicon brains of microcomputers, came soon after that.

International News System

The expanded international news system is largely an outgrowth of Western news media, especially those of Britain, America, and France. A world news system exists today because the peoples of the Western democracies wanted and needed world news, and the great independent newspapers and news agencies, and later broadcast organizations, have cooperated and competed to satisfy those wants and needs. Editors and correspondents, working for independent (that is to say, nongovernmental) news organizations, have developed the traditions and patterns of providing the almost instantaneous world news upon which people everywhere have come to rely. The credibility and legitimacy that such news generally enjoys rest on its usually unofficial and independently gathered nature. The ethic of Western journalism was summed up over 100 years ago by an editor of the *Times* of London:

> The first duty of the press is to obtain the earliest and most correct intelligence of the events of the time, and instantly, by disclosing them, to make them the common property of the nation. The duty of the journalist is to present to his readers not such things as statecraft would wish them to know but the truth as near as he can attain it.

That nineteenth-century statement represents a journalistic ideal; actual practice is often much different. Some transnational media have close, compromising ties to their governments, and all independent media are subject to varying kinds of controls from the corporate interests that own them. Nonetheless, the news media of a handful of Western nations have more freedom to report world news, and hence more credibility, than media of other nations.

Some newspaper and broadcasting organizations use their own correspondents to report foreign news, but the global workhorses and the linchpins of the world news system are the world news services — Associated Press, United Press International, Reuters, Agence France Presse, and TASS, and it is no coincidence that they come from the United States, Britain, France, and the Soviet Union. In a general sense, the great powers are the great news powers. Today, however, the continued influence of France and Britain in world news may be due more to their imperial past than to their geopolitical present.

What makes these five organizations world agencies is their capability to report news from almost anywhere to almost anywhere else. (News organizations in two other economic powers, Deutsche Press Agentur in West Germany and Kyodo News Service in Japan, approach world agency status.) Although they are sometimes perceived as dominating world news flow, the four Western agencies are definitely not in a class as economic entities with such powerful multinational corporations as Exxon or ITT. UPI has been in a shaky financial condition for two decades and recently has been teetering on the edge of bankruptcy. AFP receives a reported $65 million a year in subsidies from the French government. Reuters' regular news service has not been profitable, although its financial services, which account for 82 percent of its revenues, are exceedingly so. Only AP, which primarily serves 1,298 U.S. newspapers and 5,614 broadcasters, is financially sound. Yet AP's budget of about $122 million is small potatoes indeed compared to the scope of the giant oil companies such as Exxon, which reported $4 billion in profits for a single year.

An essential support for the world news system is provided by the estimated 120 regional and national news agencies that have emerged since World War II, especially in the Third World. UNESCO reports that national agencies in ninety sovereign countries provide their nations' newspapers and radio and television stations with domestic and foreign news. In fifty countries, the state directly controls or operates these agencies; in the forty others, one or more of the organizations are cooperatively financed and operated by newspapers of public corporations. The quality and professionalism of these news agencies differ greatly. Many are merely government information offices and do little real news gathering. Most subscribe to or have exchange agreements with one or more of the five world agencies and are the only channels within their countries to receive foreign news from the world agencies, which, in turn, distribute their domestic news abroad. Thus, by exchanging their news with world services, the small national agencies help extend the reach of the world news system.[2]

The national agencies become a vital link, especially in the Third World, between the four major world agencies and the "retail" newspapers, broadcast stations, and other recipients of the reports of AP, UPI, Reuters, and AFP. The national agencies are a source of revenue for the world agencies and distribute the news reports to local media that otherwise might not receive them.[3] Finally, the national agencies stand as key gatekeepers (and potential censors), deciding what news can and cannot be distributed to the local media.

The dominant and largest institution in the world news system is AP, a cooperative owned mainly by American newspapers. Reuters, AFP, and UPI compete with AP, often very effectively, in certain areas such as Africa, but cannot match its comprehensiveness and financial resources. Because it is part of the Soviet government structure, TASS is a special case among the world agencies and has less credibility than the other four.

Some of the great newspapers of the world — *Times, Daily Telegraph,* and *The Guardian* of London; *Le Monde* of France; *Frankfurter Allgemeine* of Germany; *Neue Zürcher Zeitung* of Switzerland; *Asahi* of Japan; *New York Times, Washington Post, Los Angeles Times,* and others in the United States — maintain their own correspondents abroad, as do the extensive broadcasting systems — BBC, CBS, NBC — as well as the news magazines — *Time, Newsweek, The Economist, L'Express, Der Spiegel.* Some of the great newspapers, such as the *New York Times, Washington Post,* and *Los Angeles Times,* syndicate their news and as a result compete as well as cooperate with the world news agencies.

However, AP's central role is undisputed. By the agency's count, more than a billion people have daily access to AP news. Like other world agencies, AP uses an extensive network of leased satellite circuits, submarine cables, and radio transmissions to supply newspapers and broadcasters with up-to-the-minute information on developments around the world twenty-four hours a day. As a result, newspapers and broadcasters in Singapore, Buenos Aires, Johannesburg, or New Delhi can publish or broadcast news bulletins simultaneously, regardless of how distant the news being reported. Three key centers—New York, London, and Tokyo—channel the millions of words and pictures transmitted daily to more than 10,000 subscribers in 110 countries. The news flows in to New York from eighty overseas bureaus staffed by 400 men and women in sixty-three countries. On a given day in the New York bureau, some 182,000 words flow in (stories, financial reports and tables, messages, other traffic) to the foreign desk, which produces 50,000 words for U.S. newspapers and other subscribers. About 87,000 words emanate from Europe, the Mideast, and Africa; another 59,000 come from Asia; and 36,000 words are filed from Latin America.[4] Without its full and free access to the news and photos of all members of the cooperative, AP would have to spend much more than the $122 million each year in news gathering (still far more than any competitor).

It has been said with some but not much exaggeration that an American's right to know is the world's right to know. For any news story that gets into the American news media can and often does flow rapidly around the world and can appear in local media anywhere if it gets by the various gatekeepers that select and reject the news of the day. So stories about hostages in Beirut, debt-ridden nations of Latin America, a hijacking of an airliner in the Middle East, a summit meeting in Geneva, an earthquake in Mexico City (or any other report prepared for the U.S. news media) can and often will be read or viewed or listened to in Africa, Asia, or Latin America. The same, of course, can be said for a story printed first in London, Paris, or Bonn.

The domination of international news by AP and other Western news media is sometimes resented by Third World and Socialist nations. Third World nations particularly are dependent on the Western agencies and media to find out about themselves and their neighbors, and they criticize what they consider a one-way flow from North to South, from the rich to the poor. Without question, there is a basis to some complaints against the Western media. But the West does not enjoy a closed monopoly of world news; any news organization is free to report world news, but few have the will or capability of doing so. Moreover, as far ranging and technically sophisticated as it is, the world's present news system is not as pervasive and efficient as it might be, considering the world's diversity and its need for information. Western journalists do an imperfect job, and most operate under a variety of constraints, which are discussed in Chapter 7. But it is the only operational news system the world has, as Martin Woollacott, *The Guardian*'s chief correspondent in Asia, has pointed out:

> For all its defects, the Western foreign press corps is all that the world has got in the way of an efficient international news gathering organization. Even in Western terms, it is a curiously unrepresentative affair, dominated as it is by the big American and British news agencies, newspapers, magazines, and broadcasting organizations. The French are in it, but are a poor second. After them trail the other Western European countries, with the Japanese foreign press, in spite of the manpower it deploys, on the periphery. This organization, whose oddities are a product of history, is, however, the only existing means of maintaining a flow of reasonably reliable information between countries. The news establishments of the Communist countries hardly offer a feasible alternative. And the occasional efforts of Asian and African countries to set up their own systems of international news gathering have all been failures. Their papers cannot afford foreign correspondents, and the few projects for Asian and African news agencies have collapsed for lack of money, expertise, and customers.[5]

History of News Distribution

The history of today's international system of news distribution is essentially the story of the world news agencies and their utilization of technological innovations. As the telegraph, cable, teletype, wireless (later radio), and communications satellites (comsats) became operational, the news agencies or "wire services" (as they were once called) employed each new device to transmit more and more news ever-more quickly from capital to capital.

Modern transnational information exchange probably had its beginnings with manuscript newletters containing political and economic information that were circulated in the late Middle Ages between the various branches of large trading companies. The sixteenth-century newsletters of the house of the Fuggers of Augsburg, Germany, were particularly well known and were read by selected outsiders involved in trade, shipping, or commerce.

The contemporary news agencies, however, evolved in nineteenth-century Europe and America. In 1835, Charles Havas, a young Frenchman of Portuguese birth, organized a service with correspondents around Europe to collect news of interest to businessmen, financiers, and diplomats. Employing semaphore signals and carrier pigeons, Havas got the news to his clients more rapidly than the usual post or special courier. Several years later, newspapers began taking advantage of the faster Havas service.

Competitors soon followed. In 1848, Bernard Wolff, a former Havas man, set up a joint news service between German and northern European papers; this later became the Wolff News Agency. Still another former Havas employee, Paul Julius Reuter, a German, established a pigeon post system to deliver the final stock prices between Brussels and Aachen, then the only gap in a telegraph system uniting the commercial centers of Berlin and Paris. After the completed telegraph link rendered this pigeon communication system obsolete, Reuter recognized that he had to be at one terminus of a cable or telegraph in order to survive. Since the Germans already controlled one end and the French the other, Reuter moved to London; when the cross-channel cable link reached the British capital in 1851, he was there to exploit it. (Reuter's Telegraph Company became known as Reuters.)

Reuters' slogan directive to "follow the cable" (which was the practice of other news agencies as well) epitomized the utilization of the world's increasing capacity in telecommunications. Reuters grew with and survived the British Empire. In the mid-1980s, Reuters operated with 670 journalists, 100 photographers, plus 1,000 stringers in 103 cities in some seventy-four countries. Reuters has expanded its operations in the United States with twelve bureaus in various U.S. cities, employing thirty-seven journalists in its Washington, D.C., offices alone.

Agence Havas became the dominant news service outside the British Empire—in France, Switzerland, Italy, Spain, Portugal, Egypt (with Reuters), and Central and South America. Following the fall of France in 1940, Agence Havas was dissolved. It was reborn in 1944 as Agence France Presse but required subsidies from the French government to survive financially. In 1957, AFP became autonomous under a controlling board that included eight directors from French newspapers, although its ties with the French government have remained close. Today, AFP, with a $90 million budget, has more than 200 staffers and more than 1,000 local employees. It serves subscribers in 160 countries, distributing news in French, English, Spanish, German, Arabic, and Portuguese.[6]

The three nineteenth-century European services were all profit-making organizations, selling their news to any newspaper willing to buy. American newspapers, finding foreign news expensive to collect, decided to cooperate rather than compete. In 1848, the leading New York papers formed the New York Associated Press to share the costs of obtaining foreign news transmitted on the newly perfected telegraph from Boston. During the remainder of the century, other regional cooperatives were formed (and some dissolved) until 1900, when the system was reorganized and incorporated in New York as the Associated Press.

Because AP members denied their service to competing papers, rival agencies were established. In 1907, E. W. Scripps organized the United Press Association to compete with AP, and William Randolph Hearst formed International News Service in 1909 to supply his own newspapers. UP bought out INS in 1958, and in recent years United Press International claimed it had 6,972 subscribers worldwide and spent about $78 million annually to collect the news it sold. Within the United States, UPI in 1985 had 800 client newspapers and 3,300 broadcast stations as against 1,260 papers and 5,700 stations for AP.[7]

However, UPI's revenues were not sufficient to cover the cost of running its worldwide network of 850 journalists in 101 domestic and sixty-five overseas bureaus. Together they produced eight million words a day for UPI's various state, national, and international wires. The agency's precarious financial situation was a subject of some concern, since most media organizations at least gave lip service to the importance of two competing U.S. news agencies here and abroad. The *Wall Street Journal* reported that UPI was losing newspaper clients and had lost millions of dollars since 1961, its most recent profitable year.[8] After several different owners failed to turn a profit, UPI management filed for protection from creditors in the U.S. Bankruptcy Court in Washington, D.C., in 1985. Its subsequent reorganization plan, submitted in April 1986, was finally approved by that court in June 1986. So the sale of the news agency for an estimated $41 million to Mexican publisher Mario Vazquez Rana, the owner of the *El Sol* chain of newspapers based in Mexico City, went through. Houston developer Joe D. Russo participated as a 10 percent partner in the financially troubled service.[9] Despite new ownership, the future of UPI remains cloudy.

Atypical among the big five global agencies is TASS, an integral part of the Soviet Union's government. Established in 1918 under the name ROSTA, TASS actively supports official Soviet policies, but operates on a worldwide basis, often supplying its service at little or no cost to media in some countries. Few papers outside the Communist orbit rely on it completely; its ties to the Soviet government undermine its credibility. TASS does provide useful and important information, however, and has exchange agreements with Western agencies.

These five agencies flowered because of an extensive root system of telegraph and submarine cables. Reuters' early dominance grew out of its accessibility to the cables linking the British Empire. The cable press rate was established at about a penny a word between points in the empire, and this markedly affected what news flowed where around the world. Wireless and shortwave radio started to weaken the importance of the cable, a process that was completed with the development of the INTELSAT communications satellite system, which can deliver the news anywhere in the world. The catch phrase of "follow the cable" was replaced by "feed the bird," a reference to the *Early Bird* communications satellite launched in 1965 and used to relay television news film across the Atlantic.

News, whether by comsat or carrier pigeon, is highly perishable, and if interest in a particular story is strong enough, it will move at incredible speed to numerous points in the world, providing there are no political or technological barriers to its transmission and reception. And it is the comsats that have made the same-day or same-hour reporting of international events on the evening television news show so commonplace.

Live feeds from another continent are easily identifiable as the work of the network involved, but the source of news on film or tape is not as evident. Most viewers are unaware that much of the foreign news on television is supplied by two television news agencies dominated by American and British interests.

Visnews, the biggest and best known, is the world's leading supplier of international news actuality material for television, servicing more than 170 broadcasters in almost every country that has a television service. Its promotional boast that Visnews reaches 99 percent of television receivers is largely true.[10] Three-quarters of Visnews shares are owned equally by Reuters and the British Broadcasting Corporation and the remaining one-quarter by public television services of Australia, Canada, and New Zealand. WTN (World Television News), the other major film agency, started as UPITN, an enterprise of UPI and Britain's Independent Television News organization; the financially troubled news agency later sold out its interest.

Visnews supplies BBC news film to the American NBC network, and it sells to the world NBC news film as well as actualities shot by BBC and Japan's NHK. The other two American networks, CBS and ABC, and the West German DPA-Etes organization also sell their domestic television news abroad.[11]

New Dimensions of International News

The international information system is rapidly moving toward that theoretical condition where it is possible to send a large amount of information everywhere almost instantly.

With the greatly enhanced technological reach of international communications, the location of a sender or receiver is no longer as important as it once was. The key gatekeepers of world news are still concentrated in New York, London, Paris, and similar metropolitan centers, but it is not necessary to be in those cities to follow the news of the world. A shortwave radio can keep a person almost anywhere in touch with the day's principal events. Furthermore, distance has become increasingly less a factor in the cost of long-distance communications, whether it be private telephone, television reception, or news reports bounced off satellites. Essentially the same technological process (and at the same cost) is required to send a news flash via satellite from London to Paris as from London to Tokyo. And the greater the use of the system, the less is the unit cost of messages sent. International communication is tied to computer technology, and in that explosive field the costs of computers are dropping as rapidly as their efficiency is increasing. In addition, the capacity of comsats to carry information is expanding.

But the implications of this greatly enhanced capability to communicate rapidly over long distances go beyond the technology and costs. Not only have speed and volume increased along with greater geographical dispersion of international news flow, but the nature and effects of the content have changed and diversified as well. Instead of mere words and numbers, color television coverage is now delivered to the world's news publics, greatly increasing the impact of the message on the audience. As a result, there is a new and significant kind of audience involvement and participation in world news events. The propaganda truism that the report of the event is as important as the event itself has greater impact than ever in the age of media events.

The fact that 600 million people around the world watched on television as Neil Armstrong stepped onto the moon may be perhaps just as important as the moon walk itself, for in those moments, the world was unified and shared a historic experience that transcended political ideology and nationality.

International television coverage of a news event can affect the political impact of the event itself. Millions in Europe in August 1969 watched live television coverage of Soviet tanks invading Czechoslovakia via a relay from Prague to Vienna and thence to the Eurovision network. Consequently, the Soviet Union was never able to convince the world that the invasion was anything other than a ruthless repression of the Dubcek regime.

On the other hand, the fact that the Western media have been largely barred from reporting the prolonged war in Afghanistan between Soviet forces and Afghan guerrillas has greatly minimized the impact of that struggle on the world's awareness. Again, if the world is unaware of an event, then for many the event has not occurred.

Similarly, the saturation television coverage of the quadrennial Olympic Games has moved that event beyond sport and into the political arena. The worldwide television audience of recent Olympics was estimated to be two billion.

Color television reportage brings us closer to events and involves us emotionally, often more than we wish. Much of the revulsion, and in time opposition, to the Vietnam War was probably a result of the repeated images on the television screen of the death and destruction in South Asian jungles. Vietnam, called "television's first war," engendered unexpected public reaction in America because of enhanced, immediate communications.

As mentioned earlier, the almost daily television pictures of rioting and violence between white police and black protesters in South Africa has directly increased the outside world's disapproval of and repugnance to apartheid and helped to make the continuing racial unrest there a major world news story. In an effort to blunt the unfavorable publicity overseas, South Africa imposed a sweeping ban on television and photographic coverage of the township violence in which more than 1,000 people, most of them black, died within fifteen months.[12]

Terrorism and Television

The very nature of television and modern mass communication that can bring people closer together while sharing the mutual grief and loss of tragic events, such as the assassination of John F. Kennedy or the funeral of Winston Churchill, also enables it to be manipulated to capture the world's attention. Unquestionably, certain acts of international terrorism, such as jet hijackings or political kidnappings and bombings, are perpetrated primarily to capture time and space in the world's media. Terrorism has been called "propaganda of the deed": violent criminal acts (often against innocent people) performed by desperate people seeking a worldwide forum for their grievances.

Of course, terrorism is not new, but the flare-ups since the 1960s—especially in the Middle East, Northern Ireland, Latin America, Turkey, Italy, and West Germany—have been caused in part, some charge, by global television coverage that beams images of terroristic violence into millions of television sets around the world. Many terrorist groups have mastered a basic lesson of this media age: television news organizations can be manipulated into becoming the final link between the terrorists and their audience, and as with all sensational crimes, the more outrageous and heinous the terrorist act, the greater attention it will receive in the world's news media. Professor Walter Laqueur has said: "The media are a terrorist's best friend. . . . Terrorists are the super-entertainers of our time."[13]

Be that as it may, terrorism *is* news, and as such it poses worrisome questions for broadcast journalists: Does television coverage really encourage and aid the terrorists' cause? Is censorship of such dramatic events ever desirable? Professor Raymond Tanter wrote: "Since terror is aimed at the media and not at the victim, success is defined in terms of media coverage. And there is no way in the West that you could not have media coverage, because you're dealing in a free society."[14]

Terrorism coverage is a journalistic problem of truly international scope, just as international terrorism itself is a transnational problem that individual nations cannot solve alone or without international cooperation. Broadcast journalists argue about whether the violence would recede if television ignored or downplayed an act of terrorism. Most doubt that self-censorship by news organizations is a good idea or even possible in such a highly competitive field; however, television organizations have established guidelines for reporting terrorism incidents in a more restrained and rational way.

HOSTAGES IN IRAN. The seizure of the U.S. embassy in Iran in November 1979, with more than fifty American citizens (virtually all diplomatic personnel) held hostage, added a new and deepening dimension to the history of terrorism and the media's increasingly blurred role as both reporter and participant.

For the first time, a sovereign government became an overt party to the terrorism by supporting instead of ousting the young militants who, in contravention of recognized international law and custom, took over an embassy compound and imprisoned its personnel. Their stated purpose was to dramatize the grievances of

Iranians against the deposed Shah Mohammad Reza Pahlavi and force the U.S. government to return him to Iran for trial. To get the U.S. media's attention (and the world's), the Iranians invited back the U.S. reporters they had previously expelled. Visas were issued, coverage was unimpeded, transmission facilities were largely unrestricted, and even interviews were granted by Ayatollah Khomeini, the leader of the new Muslim state. Most observers agree that the militants and Iran's rulers expected that the heavy print and television coverage of the outpouring of support for the terrorists by huge, demonstrating crowds around the embassy gates in Tehran would convince American and world public opinion of the justice of their cause. They had expectations, it is believed, that the dramatic pictures and reports, night after night on the evening news, would do for them what coverage of the Vietnam War and the protests against it did for the antiwar movement in the United States in the late 1960s and early 1970s.

The saturation coverage of the year's biggest story quickly engulfed the U.S. news media, especially television, in controversy and brought charges that they were being used and manipulated by the Iranian militants. Particularly controversial was an interview by NBC News with an American hostage under conditions dictated by the Iranian captors, conditions that both CBS and ABC had found unacceptable. The resulting criticism of NBC included such comments as: "NBC is the Benedict Arnold of broadcast journalism," and "The broadcast furthered the aims of Iranian terrorists." President Carter's press secretary, Jody Powell, called it "a cruel and cynical attempt" by Iran to divert public attention. NBC defended its broadcast as an "important public service."

For the more than 300 foreign journalists working in Tehran in the first months of the crisis, there was indeed a thin line between being manipulated by the Iranian militants and responding to legitimate demands from their own highly competitive news organizations and their publics at home for the latest information.

Indisputably, the Western journalists in Tehran were part of the story and, inevitably, part of the controversy. The *New York Times* editorially came to the defense of television news:

> American television, in doing its job, may at times serve Iranian Government purposes. It may at times serve American Government purposes. But throughout, it serves American *public* purposes as well. The public needs to understand Ira-

nian passions, real as well as staged. The public is not, in any
case, so gullible as to swallow any Iranian argument whole; if
anything, the various televised appearances of Iranian leaders
have strengthened American resolve. . . . American journalists have not sought a diplomatic role in Iran. It has been
thrust upon them. . . . The lesson is the same as always: the
only duty the media can effectively perform is their own.[15]

REPLAY IN BEIRUT. In June 1985, TWA
Flight 847 out of Athens was hijacked, and
its crew and passengers were held captive in Beirut. For more than
two weeks, the three U.S. networks devoted more than half their
evening news shows plus uncounted hours of unscheduled time to
the story. In most newspapers, the story was on page one from
June 15 to July 7. Indeed, the event looked like a replay of the
Iranian hostage story and one that the news business could not
ignore.

As before, television was accused of aiding and abetting the
terrorists by sympathetically publicizing their cause. Prime Minister Margaret Thatcher of Britain proposed a voluntary media code
of self-censorship during terrorist incidents. The idea was seconded
by U.S. Attorney General Edwin Meese. Fred Friendly, a former
president of CBS News, said the worst errors in coverage had been
caused by a "haphazard frenzy of competition" and the compul-
sion to obtain "exclusives." "We have to learn that they (the terrorists) watch TV. We need to get across that you can't shoot your
way onto our air," Friendly said.[16]

This time, however, a measure of restraint and responsibility
by television news was evident in some quarters. A study by William C. Adams of George Washington University found that the
ABC and CBS evening news programs differed sharply in their
handling of the almost daily interviews with hostages selected and
closely supervised by their Shiite captors. According to Adams,
ABC rarely reminded viewers of the circumstances under which the
hostages were interviewed and the conditions under which the material was provided. By contrast, CBS consistently attempted to
provide context and perspective; for example, one news broadcast
included a psychologist who analyzed the pressures on the hostages
during interviews and on another occasion discussed the captors'
strategy in providing the interviews.[17]

Despite the many specific criticisms of television's coverage of this highly emotional story, there was general agreement that such stories must be covered, but with restraint and good judgment. After it was over, the *Columbia Journalism Review* commented: "One of the tasks of journalism is to provide an assessment independent of that of the government and to stand apart from, rather than incite, the jingoism and xenophobia that spread so rapidly in situations involving the seizure of American citizens. In the Beirut hostage-taking, as in Iran, such detachment was hard to find."[18]

Tom Wicker of the *New York Times* summed it up well:

> But the real reason that television was properly present in Beirut, even at those bizarre "press conferences," is just that television exists; it has become a condition of being. It may on occasion be inconvenient, intrusive, and even harmful; but if because of government censorship or network self-censorship the hostage crisis had not been visible, *real,* on American screen, the outrage and outcry would have been a thousand times louder than what's now being heard, and rightly so; for we depend on television for perception as we depend on air for breath. And that's the way it is.[19]

The extent to which television has a responsibility for the effects of its coverage of such stories is a problem still to be resolved. Certainly, terrorism reportage highlights the fact that our ability to report a news event outdistances our ability to understand or control its impact.

Communication and Organization

A less obvious, more benign dimension of improved international communication is its capacity to *organize.* As Daniel Lerner has pointed out, communication is the neural system of organization.

> Wherever people must act together (an informal definition of organization), there they must exchange information (an informal definition of communication). Communication, in the sense of shared information, is the organizing mechanism of social actions. . . . The proposition — that communi-

cation shapes organization—is applicable to all varieties of collective behavior in social institutions: large and small, formal and informal, hierarchal and egalitarian.[20]

The ability to communicate, in other words, determines the effectiveness and the boundaries of any organization. The growth in the nineteenth century of a continental nation such as the United States would have been impossible without the telegraph and the railroad—two media of communications that "organized" an expansive hinterland. Similarly, in the last part of the twentieth century, long-distance communications—including jet air travel and some surface transport, comsats, and high-speed telecommunications—are coalescing areas of the Third World previously isolated and splintered.

Although generally poor and deficient in modern communications, the continent of Africa, for example, has been transformed in recent years by its increased ability to communicate with itself. Because of greatly expanded air travel and long-distance communications between its capitals (but still not much between a capital and adjacent hinterland), Africa is *organizing* itself. African leaders may often decry European influences on their continent, but it is precisely such "neocolonialist" influences as the BBC, INTELSAT, Air France, Reuters, *Le Monde,* AFP, *Newsweek,* British Airways, and others that have made possible the interaction and cooperation that has resulted in the Organization of African Unity and its numerous agencies and committees.

Similarly, the shared policies and activities of black Africa directed at ending white rule in South Africa would have been impossible without long-distance communications and jets. Comparable political changes throughout the world have been spawned by such communications advances, and, at the same time, new communications technology is contributing to the widening of the gap between rich and poor nations. Would there be, for instance, the same sense of common cause within the diverse Arab world stretching from Morocco to Iraq without greatly enhanced long-distance communications and jet travel?

Diffusion of Mass Culture

Another major aspect of the international communication system is its role in the diffusion of the mass culture of the West to remote parts of the world. Whether conveyed by printed word, electronic image, or recorded sound, Western motion pictures, television programs, popular music, books, video and audio cassettes, and magazines have had an impact on traditional cultures around the world that can only be described as revolutionary. To the extent that we are moving toward a rudimentary world community, it can be argued that the world is beginning to share a common mass culture based on that of the West. The traditional cultures of diverse ethnic societies and nationalities are being steadily eroded and modified by this cultural intrusion, principally from the United States and Britain. This is, of course, part of a long-term historical process that predates modern mass media, but in recent years the trend has accelerated.

For example, in a recent year, gross billings and U.S. exports of motion pictures and television programs amounted to $700 million, with movies accounting for two-thirds of the total. In the news area, over 300 newspapers outside the United States subscribed to either the New York Times or Washington Post-Los Angeles Times supplementary news services.

The dissemination of Anglo-American mass culture, especially through movies and music videos, has been greatly facilitated by the rapid dissemination of an new communications process — video cassette recordings and the equipment to play them. As expected, the penetration of video cassette recorders (VCRs) has been greatest in those countries that already have the largest number of television sets. But in the early years of this new technology, interesting differences emerged. In Western Europe in 1983, some 16,844,000 VCRs were imported for 119,222,000 television sets, or a penetration of 14.1 percent. But in the United States and Canada, with their 189,280,000 television sets, 14,426,000 VCRs were imported for a penetration rate of only 7.6 percent. On the other hand, in the eight oil-rich countries of the Persian Gulf, including Saudi Arabia, a whopping 78.5 percent of all television sets were accompanied by a VCR. It was reported that bootlegged copies of the controversial program, "Death of a Princess," was being shown on VCRs in Saudi Arabia at the same time that it was being broadcast – over the Saudi government's objections – in Britain and the United States.[21]

Why the early differences in VCR penetration? An important factor, according to Benjamin Compaine, is competition from other forms of television. In Western Europe, where there are typically two government-controlled or highly regulated television networks, VCRs permit viewers to do their own programming by renting or buying tapes. Perhaps the mass audience was showing that it was not satisfied with what broadcasting offers. In the United States, with four networks and expanding cable services, VCRs have had a healthy growth only since 1982. But by the mid-1980s, VCR use in even the choice-rich United States had multiplied, and the cassette sale and rental business expanded with a corresponding drop in total viewership of the established networks.

In Saudi Arabia, the only choice for over-the-air television is the puritanical, heavily controlled and dull programming of government television. (For example, religious orthodoxy requires that a Saudi woman's face not be shown on television.) As a result, VCRs have proliferated, and much of the viewing includes the forbidden fruit of Western movies, including X-rated films, smuggled into the country.

The Soviet Union provides another example of how VCRs are spreading Western mass culture even in societies where it is frowned on or officially banned. Video recorders appeared in the Soviet Union in the late 1970s and soon started to become a desired consumer item. Although the numbers of viewers are smaller and the cost more than in the West, increasing numbers of Russians are watching movies at home. Most films viewed are Western made and are officially banned in the Soviet Union.[22]

The initial official response was to prevent the introduction of VCRs and discourage their use. Now the Soviet government has started mass producing video players and has made available a limited number of ideologically safe films. However, officials are unable to keep home video viewing within acceptable political limits. Pornographic films, popular at first, have been supplanted by more serious films that pose a greater threat to political orthodoxy. One of the most popular films in 1985 was "Man of Iron," a Polish film that sympathetically chronicled labor unrest in Gdansk, the birthplace of the Solidarity labor movement.[23] Copies of movies from the West, available only on the black market, may sell for

200 or 250 rubles in Moscow. Such cassettes are brought into the Soviet Union by tourists, by Russians who travel abroad, and by some diplomats, whose luggage is not checked at customs. And throughout the developing nations, small shops renting or selling video cassettes from the West have become commonplace. To the American, the VCR is a convenient way to watch a movie or a music video. But to millions in non-Western nations, VCRs are a means of enjoying the otherwise prohibited products of Western mass culture, a media activity that authoritarian governments are having difficulty censoring or controlling.

This steady flow of Western entertainment has resulted in a love-hate relationship between many peoples around the world and the United States. The same persons who condemn the pervasive influence of American mass culture embrace things American — whether in dress, music, entertainment, or life-style. The young European or African intellectual who castigates America as a crass commercial influence is likely to be a fan of U.S. popular music and movies, wear jeans, and follow the shifting trends of the American youth culture.

The explosion in international news communication is directly related to major scientific developments in computer technology and electronics; here, too, most of the developments have come from the West — mainly the United States — even though science and technology are perhaps the most truly international of activities.

NOTES

1. Colin Cherry, *World Communication: Threat or Promise?* (New York: Wiley Interscience, 1971), pp. 57–58.
2. UNESCO, *World Communications* (Paris: UNESCO Press, 1975), p. 9.
3. Oliver Boyd-Barrett, *The International News Agencies* (Beverly Hills: Sage, 1980), pp. 192–93.
4. Ed Frede, "AP's Foreign News Desk — They're the Gatekeepers." *AP World,* 1985, p. 3.
5. Martin Woollacott, "Western News-gathering: Why the Third World Has Reacted," *Journalism Studies Review* 1, no. 1 (June 1976):14.
6. "Happy Birthday to Agence France-Presse," *Editor & Publisher,* Oct. 12, 1985, p. 52.
7. "Pulling Wires: UPI Files for Its Life," *Time,* May 6, 1985, p. 65.
8. *Wall Street Journal,* July 11, 1979, p. 1.
9. Alex Jones, "News Service Sale Is Approved, Ending Year in Bankruptcy," *New York Times,* June 11, 1986, p. 12.
10. Jeremy Tunstall, *The Media Are American: Anglo-American Media in the World* (London: Constable, 1977), p. 14.
11. Ibid., p. 35.

12. Peter J. Boyer, "South Africa and TV: The Coverage Changes," *New York Times,* Dec. 29, 1985, p. 1.
13. Neil Hickey, "Terrorism and Television," *TV Guide,* Aug. 7, 1976, p. 2.
14. Ibid.
15. *New York Times,* Dec. 12, 1979.
16. "Terror Coverage Is Criticized," *New York Times,* July 31, 1985, p. 3.
17. "America Held Hostage, Part II," *Columbia Journalism Review,* September/October 1985, p. 21.
18. Ibid.
19. Tom Wicker, "Not a Pseudo-Event," *New York Times,* July 9, 1985, p. 27.
20. Daniel Lerner, "Notes on Communication and the Nation State," *Public Opinion Quarterly* 37, no. 4 (Winter 1973–74):541.
21. Benjamin M. Compaine, "The Expanding Base of Media Competition," *Journal of Communication* (Summer 1985):90–91.
22. Philip Taubman, "Oh Comrade, Your Rambo Cassette," *New York Times,* Dec. 9, 1985, p. 6.
23. Ibid.

4

Communications Satellites and New Technology

It would be difficult to overstate the magnitude of change that will take place in the lives of all of us, in human history, as a result of the information revolution that has so unobtrusively taken place in our day.

—John Diebold
(authority on automation)

THE presidential election of 1920 holds a place in communication history as the first in which election results were broadcast on radio. A crackling KDKA in Pittsburgh kept a small number of devotees of the new-fangled wireless in a small area of the country up to date on the tabulations as they slowly were counted.

But for large numbers of interested voters in the remote rural regions of America far from telegraph lines, without telephones, and beyond large population centers with daily newspapers, it was two weeks before the news reached them that Warren G. Harding had defeated James M. Cox for the presidency.

Sixty-five years later, there is not a place in the United States — or in much of the world—where one cannot follow a presidential election tabulation instantaneously and, indeed, be told the winner's name even before the polls close.

The drastic differences between then and now dramatize the fact that the mechanics of delivering the news to an interested public is a significant factor in the communication process. News, particularly international news, has over the years been directly

57

affected by each new invention in communications. The telegraph, cable, telephone, and radio in turn have greatly extended the reach of foreign correspondents and world news agencies and the speed with which they can deliver news, each innovation supplementing rather than replacing earlier inventions.

The pattern continues today with communications satellites (comsats) and computer-based electronic methods of moving and storing information. Like many other institutions and organizations, the news media — newspapers, news services, broadcast stations and networks, news magazines — are being strikingly altered by the computer revolution.

In our immediate concern with how international news moves about the globe, the significant changes launched by comsats cannot be ignored. Recently there has been a quantum jump in the ability of people to talk to and see one another.

As computer technology revolutionizes the commonplace telephone network, telecommunications is becoming the world's biggest business. The industry, according to the U.S. Commerce Department, is expected to generate worldwide sales worth more than $500 billion annually by the end of the 1980s. In 1984, sales of equipment and services for circulating the world's messages and pictures (including those relating to transnational news) amounted to $325 billion.[1]

Each Western nation is trying to get its share of this new expanding world of global communications. Michel Poniatowski, a former French minister of the interior, predicted that "The nations that develop the new planetary communications will command economic and even political power in the next century as surely as the railroad building countries have dominated the last century of history."[2]

Furthermore, innovations in telecommunications may directly affect international relations and the competition between East and West. U.S. Secretary of State George Shultz told a Paris audience in March 1986, "The information revolution is shifting the balance of wealth and strength among nations, challenging established institutions and values, and redefining the agenda of international discourse."

Eastern bloc leaders face an agonizing choice. "They can either open their societies to the freedom necessary for the pursuit of technological advance," Shultz said, "or they risk falling further behind the West." The development of information technology—computers, videotapes, satellite transmissions, direct-dial telephones, and the like—"not only strengthens the economic and political position of democracies: It provides a glimmer of hope that the suppressed millions of the unfree world will find their leaders forced to expand their liberties."[3]

Our concern here is with the impact of telecommunications on international news flow. And the most immediate short-term effect of comsats is a reduction in the cost of long-distance communications and a corresponding increase in the amount of words, data, and pictures exchanged. In other words, more news will flow at less expense. The more dramatic changes are in long-distance telephone calls; they form the bulk of traffic on the INTELSAT system, which is operated by a multinational consortium controlling long-distance point-to-point comsat communications. According to the 1986 Statistical Abstract of the United States, the annual number of overseas calls went from 700,000 in 1950 to 7.5 million in 1965 and then with the aid of comsats zoomed to 369.5 million by 1983. By projecting current trends, within a few years an expected billion overseas telephone calls a year will be placed in the United States; and a call halfway around the world will cost the same as a call next door and be made almost as easily.

Another short-term but profound result, as both Peter Goldmark and Arthur Clarke have predicted, is that comsats, in combination with broadcast and cable television, will permit people to live where they please, regardless of their work. When cheap, dialed conversations via color television, along with interactive computers, become commonplace, every home can be transformed into an office, theater, or classroom by pressing a few buttons.

In Clarke's view, such cheap communications will reverse the growth of the city. For him, the impact of comsats is a "slow but irresistible dispersion and decentralization of mankind. Megalopolis may soon go the way of the dinosaur."[4]

A projection of Professor Robert Jastrow is more chilling in the long term:

> The new satellites will provide a nervous system for mankind, knitting the members of our species into a global society. There are pluses and minuses. On the one hand, many lives will no doubt be enriched by freer exposure to ideas and people. Through the reduction of barriers of fear and suspi-

cion between nations, there may be greater political stability. On the other, a unified global society will be a social organism of great collective power, in which the individual plays the role of one biological cell in a complex organism. Just as a cell cannot migrate from, say, the brain to the liver, the freedom of the individual will tend to be restricted in the new society.

The last comparable change in the history of life occurred several billion years ago, when multi-celled animals evolved out of colonies of individuals. The prospect is not pleasant. But the transformation, if it occurs, will take place slowly. Those now living will be dead before it is completed and most of our descendents will be conditioned to accept their more restricted options.[5]

Whether or not we agree with Jastrow's somber view of the future, it is a reminder that people never fully appreciate the impact of new communications technology when it first appears. Clarke dismisses the notion that comsats are merely an extension of existing communications devices and will not engender much change. He places comsats in the same class as the atomic bomb and automobile, "which represent a kind of quantum jump which causes a major restructuring of society." Clarke recalled a parliamentary commission in England a hundred years ago when the chief engineer of the post office was asked to comment on the need for the latest American invention, the telephone. The engineer made this remarkable reply: "No, Sir. The Americans may have need of the telephone—but we do not. We have plenty of messenger boys."[6]

That telephone, in time, came to have its own revolutionary impact on modern life, and the personal letter has been replaced by the long-distance call. And telephone services, as has been noted, constitute the primary activity today of comsats and are the major source of revenue for INTELSAT. At the end of the 1970s, the traffic of INTELSAT was still mostly people talking to people, but by 1986, according to INTELSAT officials, at least half the information volume was machines communicating with other machines. In future years, machines will be doing more and more of the "talking." The telephone is expected to continue to be a major tool of news gathering around the world for the rest of the century, but the comsat, as a by-product of the space age, has made a more dramatic entry into our lives than did the telephone.

Journalist Brenda Maddox warned:

> It is easy to idealize and even to anthropomorphize the communications satellite. The usual kind of satellite rides 22,300 miles above the Equator, virtually equidistant from every country and every person within its enormous range. Only three are necessary to make a single television audience out of almost the entire globe. So small and so high, it seems to vault over the past, over mountains and oceans, and invites the whole world, jungle and suburb, to speak through it. The symbolic power of the satellite is so great that it is believed to have almost magical powers to educate, almost diabolical powers to persuade. The deep feelings that the device has aroused have bedeviled its short life. Planning for its orderly and effective use has been difficult and may become more so.[7]

Although they have been called microwave relay towers in the sky, comsats do have broader, unique properties. They do not link just two points, but many. They can receive from many places at the same time and transmit to many more, sending a panoply of message forms at once—television, telephone, telex, photo facsimile, and high-speed computer data. For example, an increased mobility of money is a result of the computer revolution. Computers and comsats have created a global financial marketplace, and it has been estimated that during a single working day, "bits" of information about financial transactions representing as much as $100 billion is in transit along with all the rest of the traffic moving via satellite between Europe and North America.

Further, with comsats, distance is not a factor in the cost. Communications between Tokyo and Seattle, about 5,000 miles, and communications between Seattle and Portland, 175 miles, require identical facilities: two earth stations and a satellite. Irrelevant as well are the historic patterns of the world's communications, which were once channeled through the capital cities of the former colonial powers, all in the Northern Hemisphere. A telephone call from one African country to another had to go through London or Paris or both. In Latin America, a call between countries often had to go through New York or even London.

International journalism has benefited greatly from the developments that have made satellites an integral part of the communications industry. Today, satellite systems are operational at the international (intercontinental) level, the regional (continental) level, and the domestic (national) level. In addition, numerous specialized systems are functioning, such as those designed for military, data relay, maritime, and aeronautical purposes.[8] As a result of the endeavors of dozens of laboratories and hundreds of scientists and engineers, some 1,400 satellites were out in space in 1985.[9]

INTELSAT is the largest and oldest system; some 112 nations, each with its own earth segment, belong to the consortium, and any two member countries can communicate directly without going through former colonial capitals.[10] User countries, territories, and possessions total about 170, operating internationally on almost 1,500 preassigned pathways. INTELSAT also functions as the carrier for national domestic services in twenty-seven countries (Algeria, Argentina, Chile, China, Colombia, Denmark, India, Iran, Italy, Libya, Malaysia, Morocco, Mozambique, Niger, Nigeria, Norway, Oman, Peru, Portugal, Saudi Arabia, Spain, South Africa, Sudan, Thailand, United Kingdom, Venezuela, and Zaire).

In acquiring regional comsat systems, the developed nations (North America, Western Europe, and Japan) were moving at a much faster rate than those of the Third World. Still there has been significant progress among the poorer nations, which lack terrestrial telecommunications systems and so stand to gain much from regional comsats. Far-flung Indonesia with its thousands of islands has been moving ahead with its *PALAPA 1* and *2* satellites. In June 1985, the shuttle *Discovery* launched the *ARABSAT,* a satellite that will serve as a space switchboard for telephone and data transmission and community television for twenty-two Arab League members from Morocco to Iraq. The same *Discovery* flight also launched the *Morelos-A,* Mexico's first satellite.

And in 1983, another U.S. space shuttle, *Challenger,* launched the *Insat 1-B* (Indian National Satellite). Built by Indian scientists at a cost of $130,000,000, the comsat has the capability of land-based telecommunications that would have cost a trillion dollars. *Insat 1-B* places 70 percent of the Indian population within range of television signals and is being used primarily for telephone services, weather forecasting, nationwide linking of computer services such as transport and tourism, and, interestingly, providing community television services to thousands of Indian villages.[11]

Television transmissions via comsats were accelerating at such a fast clip in the United States that satellite dish antennas, which only recently were curiosities of the space age, have become commonplace across America. In September 1985, 60,000 were sold each month, and industry officials predicted that the 1.2 million dish systems then installed would multiply to ten million by 1990. In 1980, a good dish installation cost between $10,000 and $20,000; in 1985, similar dishes sold for less than $5,000. General Satellite of Slinger, Wisconsin, offered a "complete backyard system" for only $370.[12]

Dishes can intercept a range of programming far exceeding even the offerings of the most complete cable systems, catching signals from as many as 150 broadcasters. Myriad economic, technical, and legal problems involving copyright, invasion of privacy, pirating, and the like, have resulted. Pay-television services and superstations now scramble their signals, requiring dish owners to pay the services or stations for unscrambling devices. Nevertheless, these dish antennas mean that remote areas, from the hills of Appalachia to the arctic wastes of northern Canada, can now receive a variety of television services previously available only in population-dense areas. And these great technological advances in direct broadcast satellites, including the dropping price for receivers, foretell the potential of such equipment throughout the Third World, especially when combined with cable systems.

International News
by Comsats

Comsats have greatly expanded the capacity of the news media to move international news around the globe, but it is the ability of the satellites to relay color television signals (giving that medium an international impact) that has made comsat technology such a significant mass communication development. This is true even though television use accounts for a comparatively small proportion of the monthly revenue of INTELSAT.

When *Early Bird,* the first commercial comsat, was launched in 1965, the principal television use was expected to be for occasional live events such as sports, state funerals, and space missions and the coverage of disasters and wars. While reportage of such major events still accounts for much television traffic on INTELSAT, the most extensive and consistent use of the global system is for daily television news packages sent from one country to another.

The U.S. networks—NBC, CBS, and ABC—almost daily incorporate satellite news feeds from their correspondents in various parts of the world or for sporadically purchased special coverage from foreign broadcast agencies such as Visnews or WTN.

Spain and Mexico are linked full time by satellite on a channel leased jointly by the two countries, and Spanish Television (TVE) in Madrid also transmits ten or fifteen minutes of news on weekdays to broadcasters in Argentina, Brazil, Chile, Colombia, and Venezuela. When events warrant, those countries send news by satellite back to TVE under what has come to be known as the Ibero-American News Exchange. Telediffusion France (TDF) in Paris sends a daily package of news to Israel, Iran, Jordan, Martinique, the Ivory Coast, Gabon, Senegal, Zaire, French Guiana, Kuwait, and Saudi Arabia. In London, Visnews provides a daily news transmission to Australia using the Indian Ocean satellite.

Comsats and computer-based data transmissions have also greatly enhanced the capacity of the world news services to move written news around the world. Comsats have become an important supplementary—perhaps approaching the primary—channel along with cable, radio telephone, telegraph, and telex to disseminate major news. As a result, the international news flow, moving via electronic impulses from computer to computer at ever-greater speeds, has markedly increased in volume. An Associated Press correspondent in Moscow can type a story into a video display terminal in AP's Moscow bureau, and the story can appear via comsat almost simultaneously on VDT screens in Paris, London, New York, Tokyo, Johannesburg, and Rome.

In today's worldwide news communication, a straight line is not the quickest route between two points. Take, for example, a major AP news story breaking in Kuala Lumpur, Malaysia. Say it involves a top Japanese personality, making it an important story in Tokyo, but also of interest in the United States and elsewhere. The AP correspondent writes the story, and before the operator finishes transmitting the 200-word urgent lead from Kuala Lumpur via teleprinter, the story is being received in Tokyo and by AP members around the world.

Here is how the story is routed: Kuala Lumpur has an AP telephone circuit that carries the story southeast to Singapore.

From there is is automatically relayed northward via undersea cable to Hong Kong. Autorelay moves it again by undersea cable southeast to Manila, then eastward to a cablehead in San Francisco, and by overland relay to New York. Circuit delay—i.e., lapsed time—is just one second. At New York it is available to the AP "A" wire and for overseas relay to Europe. Then, a New York computer turns the story around and sends it back via land lines and microwave relay to the earth-satellite relay station at Marysville, California. From there it is bounced off an INTELSAT satellite parked above the equator 22,500 miles over the Gilbert Islands in the South Pacific. The downward bounce from the comsat carries the story into Tokyo, seconds from the time it was transmitted from Kuala Lumpur. The story has traveled halfway around the world eastward and back again westward, racing from tropical Malaysia to wintry New York to the equator and then to chilly Tokyo.

AP's high-speed delivery of news, typical of the world services, has expanded steadily since 1961 when the old slow-speed barrier was broken by its DataSpeed transmissions of stock market tables at 1,050 words per minute. Faster delivery of general news copy began in 1975 with AP DataStream, which transmits 1,200 words per minute directly into clients' computers for entry into electronic editing systems. Then in May 1976, AP inaugurated a new service, AP DigitalStocks, which transmitted ten times faster than any existing system—12,000 words per minute. These new digital circuits transferred stock market tables from computer to computer, thus eliminating tape and the personnel to handle it in newspaper backshops. Such methods can move general as well as financial news across oceans as easily as across continents.

In February 1985, AP became the first user of a new high-speed satellite service linking, via INTELSAT 5, New York and London, perhaps the world's two major news centers. AP uses three circuits to carry news, photo, and financial services. Only two years before, AP announced that its own news service between London and New York was upgraded to 300 words per minute. With the new link, AP has the equivalent of six feeds of 12,000 words per minute on each circuit.[13]

Also in 1985, AP put into operation at its New York headquarters a new "electronic ear," a fifteen-foot dish antenna that can pick up satellite transmissions from AP earth stations anywhere in the

United States. Once received by the new antenna, signals are fed via cables into AP headquarters processing by computer. Outgoing transmissions are then routed via landlines and microwave to Western Union in Glenwood, New Jersey, and beamed to an orbiting satellite for relay to the appropriate AP earth receiving station.[14]

The individual daily newspaper receiving this rapidly disseminated material has been undergoing a parallel technological revolution based on computer technology and electronic data handling. The whole process of producing a daily newspaper has been speeded by moving electrons instead of words on paper. Typewriters, editing pencils, and paper have virtually disappeared from many newsrooms. A reporter now writes a news story on a video display terminal, which stores it in a computer until an editor calls it up at will onto his or her own VDT for editing. When the story is ready for printing, the editor presses a VDT key, and the story goes to electronically controlled machines that set it in type. Most daily newspapers can receive and process far greater amounts of editorial copy more quickly and at less expense than ever before. AP and UPI reports go directly into computers in newspaper offices. Hence the capacity to handle and print more international news, if editors are disposed to do so, has expanded.

The speed and scope of foreign news reporting is constantly widening as the use of portable VDTs is increasing. Foreign correspondents have long said that their worst problems are not censorship or other authoritarian restraints, but communications — getting to the remote news scene, such as an earthquake in Peru or a civil war in Angola, and then getting the story out. The technology to solve part of that problem has been developed and increasingly utilized, especially small portable computers that can transmit stories over phone lines directly to newsroom systems. Initially, these portables were used to cover golf matches, auto races, football and basketball games, and court trials, but now they are utilized for the whole range of news events.

Another communication innovation that promises to be useful to the foreign reporter in the field is a portable wireless telephone. Brenda Maddox predicts that of the estimated $640 billion that the world will spend on telecommunications equipment in the next decade, a good share will go for mobile radio, including satellite-borne maritime communications, air-to-ground services, and a limitless variety of automobile and carry-along telephones. The growth of mobile communications will be aided by the increasing sophistication of cellular radio, which opens the possibility of a telephone on every wrist and a personal telephone number. Such communication technology has obvious advantages for the reporter in the field.[15] This means an editor can telephone a foreign correspondent whether he or she is covering a conference in Geneva or an election in the Philippines. And that correspondent could, if necessary, send in the story by his or her cordless telephone.

Facsimile Newspapers

A further utilization of comsats that promises to be more momentous is facsimile production and distribution of national and international newspapers. The *Wall Street Journal* pioneered in this technology, which may profoundly alter the structure of the daily newspaper business. This is the way it works: the *Journal* is put together at a production plant in Chicopee, Massachusetts. A fascimile of each page is then transmitted electronically to a satellite 22,300 miles above the equator. The satellite relays the page data to a *Journal* printing plant in, say, Orlando, Florida, where it is received on page-sized photographic film. The sending and receiving of data transmitted on equipment designed by American Satellite Corporation takes about three minutes. Once the fascimile data is received, the photographic film is processed into offset plates. These plates then are placed on a newspaper press that can print up to 70,000 issues an hour for distribution in Florida and other parts of the Southeast. The identical process occurs in a total of twelve printing plants serving the Midwest, Southwest, and West Coast regional editions. The *Wall Street Journal* has extended this expertise to Asia (see Chap. 5), and further expansion of the entire Dow Jones network (which includes the *Wall Street Journal*) is under way. This kind of technological innovation, plus an informative, well-written news product, has moved the *Wall Street Journal* into first place in circulation among U.S. dailies — 1,985,559 as of March 31, 1986.[16]

Another, more recent national daily newspaper, the Gannett company's *USA TODAY* has utilized the same facsimile production methods, circulating 1,168,222 copies from thirty U.S. printing sites.[17] In October 1985, *USA TODAY* began beaming facsimile pages of its international edition to Singapore for printing and distribution in the Far East. Previously, its international edition circulated only in Europe and parts of the Middle East via an airlift from a printing site in the United States.

Other publications routinely utilize facsimile transmission technology. The national edition of the *New York Times* (1,035,426 total circulation in 1986) is printed in several regions of the United States to facilitate its same-day delivery across the nation. The *World Journal,* a Chinese-language daily newspaper in New York City, is partially composed in New York and printed in San Francisco the same day. Again, full pages are transmitted via American Satellite network in minutes, and essentially the same paper is read by readers 3,000 miles apart.

Comsats are not necessary for facsimile production between distant points if surface means exist to handle the high-data-rate transmission necessary for high-speed facsimile movement. A famous Italian daily, the *Corriere Della Sera* of Milan, has a high-speed terrestrial system that can transmit full-page, high-resolution proofs in six minutes or less per page from Milan to a subsidiary printing plant in Rome.

As early as 1974, the Paris-based *International Herald Tribune* began transmitting nightly the fourteen to sixteen pages of the newspaper to printers in Uxbridge, England, for printing and distribution in the United Kingdom. The transmission system was billed at the time as the first to cross national borders.

Such developments make the truly international or worldwide newspaper a technical reality, and in the foreseeable future, daily newspapers with a cosmopolitan outlook, such as the *Times* of London, *New York Times, Wall Street Journal, Le Monde* of Paris, or the *International Herald Tribune,* will be available via comsat instead of by mail to readers in widely scattered places. In time, truly global daily publications could appear.

Is the Daily Newspaper Becoming Obsolete?

These fast-moving changes in media technology raise the prospect that the daily newspaper—words printed on paper—itself may be headed for extinction. With the development of microcomputerization, the personal computer, and the television set, either together or separately, can become a kind of home encyclopedia, spewing out an almost limitless amount of written information including the day's news. Already in use in Europe and America are two major systems, called teletext and viewdata, that can electronically deliver news and information.

Teletext utilizes the fact that the television broadcast signal that delivers a picture to a set does not use all the 525 lines of spectrum available. Twenty-one of the unused lines are harnessed by a central computer to transmit all kinds of written messages. Such data are invisible on the screen until the viewer employs a hand-held decoder to punch up teletext in place of usual programming. An example of teletext is the CEEFAX system developed by the BBC. CEEFAX permits any subscriber to call up a particular page of news onto his or her television screen at any time. Each page (a full television screen) can contain up to 120 words. The CEEFAX system has the capacity of 100 pages, but it can be adapted to transmit an unlimited number.

The CEEFAX operation begins in the news broadcast center. There, 120-word pages of news are assembled and typed into an electronic storage device. Each of the words on the page and the page number are digitally encoded automatically. The pages are then automatically transmitted sequentially in the blank spectrum space of a normal British television broadcast. Sixty-four pages of code take approximately fifteen seconds to transmit and are repeated constantly four times a minute, hour after hour. Any or all the pages can be updated almost instantaneously. At the receiving end, in a home or office, the viewer can select any page desired. When the user punches, for example, page 23, the device waits until the next time page 23 is broadcast (maximum waiting time, fifteen seconds), then displays it on the screen. Type size is about 18 point, and the page can be held on the screen as long as the viewer wishes.

Commercial teletext services are now operating in Great Britain, Sweden, Austria, and Belgium. More than 770,000 decoders have been installed, and market penetration is 2.3 percent in those four countries. In the United States, CBS and PBS and two large publishers, Time and Field, have experimented with teletext.[18]

Viewdata, on the other hand, employs personal computers and telephone lines rather than television broadcasting to deliver information. And it is much more personalized; the viewdata customer can call up any specific information desired.

Millions of American and European households are now

equipped with perfect receivers for "electronic newspapers," as viewdata is sometimes called. Hundreds of thousands of people today use personal computers, modems, and telephones to gain almost instant access not only to the information any newspaper provides but much more. (In early 1986, the NEXIS news retrieval service began publishing the complete text of the *Los Angeles Times* in electronic form. The NEXIS data base is available to subscribers through computer terminals and carries more than 140 international newspapers, magazines, wire services, and newsletters.) This technology already enables users to do their banking, pay bills, order from catalogs, make airline reservations, buy stocks, purchase theater tickets, use an electronic encyclopedia, look up current sports scores, and many other things twenty-four hours a day without ever leaving home.

Newspapers, however, are still cheaper; furthermore, these computer services have not, so far, successfully delivered advertising. Nevertheless, one expert, Alan Horton, thinks newspaper editors would be foolish to ignore videotext's appeal today and its potential tomorrow. "Videotext technology is evolving so rapidly that almost anything that can be imagined, can be delivered," he said.[19]

Most videotext customers are served by local and regional as well as national systems, including big operations like Dow Jones News/Retrieval, CompuServe, and Source. These enterprises, major newspapers, and other Fortune 500 companies have invested hundreds of millions of dollars in videotext.[20]

Both teletext and viewdata have the potential of, if not replacing the daily newspaper, at least supplementing it. A notable difference from the traditional print and broadcast media is that the recipient or the "reader" seeks out specific news and information rather than passively receiving it. Such "information seeking" has important political and social implications for the future of mass communication.

These systems also have significance for international news. For in this era of long-distance telecommunications, an individual or a news medium can be located almost anywhere and still be able to request and obtain specific news and information from many miles away, even across distant national frontiers. And much of this information is difficult for governments, even authoritarian governments, to monitor and control.

But will such electronic information systems be a serious threat to conventional newspaper publishing? A study by the Arthur D. Little Company determined they will not be a threat in this decade, but by the mid-1990s they could substantially affect the news industry. Whether the impact is threat or opportunity will depend largely on the publishers, the study concluded. Those able to break away from their traditional roles as newspaper and magazine publishers and become broad-based "information providers" will find important additional channels for marketing their news and information services.

Implications of Rapid Change

To summarize, these innovations in communications technology suggest certain broad trends for transnational journalism:

1. The unit cost of international transmission of news will continue to drop as usage of the world news systems increases and efficiency, speed, and reach of the hardware become greater.

2. Technology is making it possible to send and receive news and other essential information almost anywhere in the world.

3. The two-way capability of cablevision, tied in with comsats and personal computers, means that information users can seek out or request specific kinds of information or news and not remain a passive mass audience.

The two-way capability of telecommunications means that a two-way flow of information, with consumers having more choice about what they receive, is more likely. The trend toward such interactive communications systems is clear.

4. Because of technical improvements, the potential number of channels and sources of information is virtually unlimited, and the possible varieties and kinds of future communication stagger the imagination.

5. A gradual merger of the science and technology of computers and communications has been taking place. In fact, a new term, "compunications," has been coined to reflect this reality.

6. These personalized communications, typified by teletext, viewdata, video cassettes, and cablevision, present a challenge to authoritarian governments, which traditionally control their news-

papers and broadcasting. How does Big Brother stop someone from watching a pirated video cassette or from calling up distant information on a home computer?

7. So far, this communications (or compunications) revolution is essentially taking place in the West, principally the United States, Japan, and Western Europe. These "information societies," all in the rich, industrialized North, are widening the already broad information gap between themselves and the Third World. A highly industrialized nation like Japan can utilize any new technology much faster than, say, Kenya, and as a result the resentments of the Third World over information inequities are exacerbated. The poorer nations want the new communications technology but lack the social and economic bases needed to use it. For many of the poor, debt-ridden nations of the Third World, sophisticated and expensive electronic systems are out of reach. Such factors only add to the deep rift between the haves and have-nots of the world, a condition many consider the greatest of all global problems.

Concerned persons here and abroad are pondering the implications of all this. American newspaper publishers and other U.S. media people formed the International Press Telecommunications Council to help assure the news media access to communications satellites. IPTC, which has British and Canadian members as well, has been concerned that new developments in computer-controlled data transmissions might increasingly restrict press telecommunications and international news flow in the years ahead.

John Forrest, IPTC chairman, told the group:

> One of the greatest problems facing both developed and developing societies is the great speed at which the technologies of the computer and communications are advancing. With the great mass of information that can now be assembled, processed, and disseminated through the technologies of the computer and modern telecommunications, mankind is now faced with the problem of having more and more facts in shorter and shorter periods of time.
>
> The advancing technologies of the developed societies are possibly now creating the seeds—I will not say of their own destruction—but are certainly creating massive problems for the societies which are developing the technologies. This especially applies to news dissemination.[21]

Society, in short, faces the danger of computer/communications technologies advancing faster than our ability to develop methods of controlling and utilizing them for the general welfare. This has always been true of technologies, but today that gap is becoming ominously wide.

NOTES

1. Joseph Fitchett, "Europe Sits by the Phone, Awaiting a Revolution," *International Herald Tribune,* Dec. 4, 1985, p. 1.
2. Ibid.
3. "Stanford Conference in Paris Attracts 500: Shultz Speaks," *Stanford Observer,* April 1986, p. 7.
4. Arthur Clarke, "Beyond Babel: The Century of the Communication Satellite," in *The Process and Effects of Mass Communication,* ed. W. Schramm and D. Roberts (Urbana: University of Illinois Press, 1971), pp. 952–65.
5. *New York Times,* June 9, 1974, News of the Week in Review section, p. 6.
6. Clarke, ibid.
7. Brenda Maddox, *Beyond Babel: New Directions in Communications* (Boston: Beacon Press, 1972), pp. 65–66.
8. Rolf T. Wigand, "The Direct Satellite Connection: Definitions and Prospects," *Journal of Communication* 30, no. 2 (Spring 1980):140–41.
9. John Barbour, "The Remarkable Evolution of Satellites," *AP Newsfeatures Report,* Aug. 19, 1985, p. 1.
10. See Marcellus Snow, "Arguments for and against Competition in International Satellite Facilities and Services: A U.S. Perspective," *Journal of Communication* (Summer 1985):51–79.
11. William K. Stevens, "India TV Boom, Reruns and Politics," *New York Times,* Sept. 27, 1984, p. 5.
12. "TV Mushrooms in the Backyard," *Time,* Sept. 16, 1985, p. 56.
13. "AP Is First User of New Service Linking New York – London," *AP Log,* Feb. 25, 1985.
14. "AP Installs Powerful, New 'Electronic Ear,' " *AP Log,* June 10, 1985, p. 1.
15. Brenda Maddox, "The Telecommunications Revolution," *World Press Review,* Dec. 1981, p. 22.
16. ABC totals quoted in *Editor & Publisher,* May 10, 1986, p. 19.
17. Ibid.
18. R. Glenn McCutchen, "Teletext Could Be THE New Technology," *Presstime,* December 1982, p. 11.
19. Alan Horton, "Videotext Ventures Explore Possible Paths to a 'Newspaper of the Future,' " *ASNE Bulletin,* Oct. 1985, p. 8.
20. Ibid.
21. Earl Wilken, "IPTC Considers Flexing Political Muscle," *Editor & Publisher,* June 4, 1977, p. 14.

5

Internationalizing the World's News Media

> Mankind has become one, but not steadfastly one as communities or even as nations used to be, nor united through years of mutual experience . . . nor yet through a common native language, but surpassing all barriers, through international broadcasting and printing.
>
> — *Alexander Solzhenitsyn*

As the international flights landed in various capitals in West Africa on Thursdays, one of the first cargoes unloaded were bundles of the international editions of *Time* and *Newsweek*. Within hours, the magazines had been distributed to news kiosks and hotel newsstands and into the hands of scores of newsboys who hawked them on street corners and in cafes and bars.

By Friday morning, virtually all had been sold. They were much in evidence at the numerous gathering places in the cities, being read not merely, as one would expect, by white tourists or resident expatriates, but by equal, often greater, numbers of local citizens as well.

This weekly event is repeated today in the countries with sufficient foreign exchange to afford it, not just in West Africa. It takes place in East Africa, too, and in similar ways in other cities around the globe—Asia, South America, Europe. Nor is the exclusive product *Time* and *Newsweek*. On Sunday afternoons in anglophonic Africa, for instance, the newsboys most likely would be selling the Sunday papers from London: the *Sunday Times,* the *Sunday Telegraph,* and the *Observer.*

The appetite for such Western publications (most of them in English, which is becoming a sort of lingua franca of international communication) is just one example of how all the major institutions of news communication — world news services, broadcast systems, great newspapers and magazines — have become internationalized in recent years. This change is the result in some instances of new technology and in others of shifting social and political realities. Whatever the cause, the fact is that more and more of the activities of the major news media now transcend parochial concerns and serve broader transnational purposes.

As worldwide institutions, the international news media share many of the attributes of multinational corporations, which have become such a powerful force in the world economy. The power and reach of these multinational corporations has been a matter of much concern, largely because they appear to be exploiting certain nations and regions at the expense of others. Yet the burgeoning activities of such giants as Exxon, General Motors, Shell, Phillips, ITT, British Petroleum, Volkswagen, the great Japanese corporations, and lesser conglomerates are a creative and predictable response to the economic opportunities presented by the interdependent world in which we live. Currently, in fact, most nations, cognizant of the investment and employment-generating potential, court multinational corporations. The solution is not just to curtail them but to regulate their activities in the interests of all. But without effective world government or even much international economic cooperation, effective regulation will be difficult, if not impossible, to accomplish.

Inability to regulate the world's economy equitably is another indication of the inadequacy of the nation state to deal with the world's truly international concerns.

The same kind of criticism leveled at multinationals is often directed at some transnational media. Charges have been made, for example, that great Western media institutions are becoming giant, profit-grubbing, multinational corporations exploiting poorer nations by dominating the news flow and dumping on them mass culture artifacts — television programs, movies, pop music records, video cassettes, magazines, and books — that disrupt local traditional cultures in the process. Included among such transnational media entrepreneurs would appear to be the U.S. television networks ABC, CBS, and NBC; the U.S. news agencies Associated Press and United Press International; Britain's British Broadcasting Corporation and Reuters; France's Agence France Presse; and surely the popular and much-imitated *Newsweek* and *Time* as well as the major motion picture and television distribution organizations.

Whether their activities are "good" or "bad" usually depends on the critic's personal tastes and ideology. But the internationalization of news media is proceeding in response to the needs of a shrinking world. The transnational media are doing more than seizing the opportunities for greater profits from new markets, though those factors are obviously important. Whether viewed as another example of Western "media imperialism" or as a significant contribution to global understanding, the international media are becoming increasingly cosmopolitan, speaking English, and catering to an internationally minded audience concerned about world problems.

"An American in Paris"

The daily, ink-on-newsprint newspaper is still the central institution of modern journalism, and there are more than 8,000 dailies worldwide. A few of the more serious "prestige" papers attract readers far beyond their national borders. Not many Americans read foreign publications, so they are unaware of the extent to which people abroad depend on newspapers and magazines published in other countries. The intellectual *Le Monde* of Paris, famous for its analyses of world affairs, is widely read in the Arab world and francophone Africa. Britain's *Guardian* and *Financial Times* are found on many foreign newsstands, as are the *Frankfurter Allgemeine* and the *Neue Zürcher Zeitung*. For example, the *Neue Zürcher Zeitung,* which celebrated its two hundredth anniversary in 1980, has a circulation of 120,000, about 20,000 of the total being copies sold outside Switzerland. Most of the paper's earnings are reinvested in the editorial department, which explains how a paper of that modest size can support thirty-three full-time foreign correspondents.

But the newspaper that has evolved furthest toward becoming a truly international daily is the *International Herald Tribune* of Paris. The *IHT* is the sole survivor of a number of English-language papers, including the *Chicago Tribune, Daily Mail* (of London), *New York Herald-Tribune,* and *New York Times,* that earlier published Paris or European editions for English-speaking travelers. Started by James Gordon Bennett in 1887 as the Paris edition of the *New York Herald,* the *IHT* has outlived its parent and today is jointly owned by Whitney Communications, the *Washington Post,* and the *New York Times.* The *IHT* is produced by an editorial staff of forty, including copyboys and clerks. About 90 percent of its copy comes from staffers on the *New York Times, Los Angeles Times, Washington Post,* and the news services. Averaging about sixteen pages a day, the *IHT* in 1986 sold 168,189 copies a day in 164 countries, and no single country accounted for more than 15 percent of the total. This marvel of distribution appears daily on some 8,500 newsstands all over Europe, supplied by editions printed in Paris, London, the Hague, Marseilles, and Zurich.

In early 1982, the *IHT* extended its fascimile transmissions to printing plants in Asia, first in Hong Kong and then in Singapore.[1] African subscribers are served by mail. On March 10, 1986, the *IHT* began printing in Miami to facilitate distribution in North America, Latin America, and the Caribbean. As editors and compositors complete their work in Paris each evening, an electronic image of each page is sent via INTELSAT V-A comsat to each of the eight printing plants at a speed of about four minutes per page. The *IHT* thus became the first newspaper in history to print the same edition simultaneously on all continents.

Although it remains an American newspaper in outlook and perspective, it has gradually acquired an important non-American readership. Nearly half its readers are an elite group of European internationalists — businesspeople, diplomats, and journalists fluent in English. These readers see the *IHT,* as do many Americans, as a superior newspaper: informative, balanced, literate, and well edited.

International Information Elite

These non-American readers are part of what William Read and other researchers have identified as an "international information elite" who, regardless of geographic location, share a similar rich fund of common experience, ideas, ways of thinking, and approaches to dealing with international problems. A U.S. Information Agency (USIA) survey found, for example, that "on the average as many as 15 to 30 percent of selected elite audiences in non-Communist countries read *Time*."[2]

Read noted: "So when American media play an agenda-setting role globally, the effect can be to assign the degree to which international attention is focused on the issue. The energy crisis during the winter of 1973–74 dramatically demonstrated what can happen. When the Arabs turned off the oil in 1973, the whole world acted like a single short-term market because of simultaneous news coverage reaching people everywhere nearly simultaneously."[3]

USIA research concludes that the "information elites" have similar clusters of interests, principally international affairs and economics. To a lesser degree, they are concerned also about social problems but do not share a high interest in art and popular culture. The research indicates a "preference for substantially useful information related to a two-tiered world: global interdependence in politics and economics balanced against global diversity in cultural preferences."[4] A salient feature of the transnational elite audiences, Read wrote, is that they sit atop indigenous societies that are, in the main, highly nationalistic.

Numerous other publications, particularly magazines, have reached and helped shape this international information elite. The prime success story of transnational magazines is, of course, *Reader's Digest,* which established its first foreign edition in Britain in 1938. In time came thirty-nine national editions printed in sixteen languages. Almost 30 million copies a month are sold abroad.[5] In some countries, including nearly all Spanish-speaking countries, *Reader's Digest* was *the* most popular magazine.[6] So successful has been its adaptation to foreign soil that many readers are unaware that the *Digest* is not an indigenous publication. Although studies show that *Digest* readers abroad belong to a "quality audience" of the affluent, the well educated, and the well informed, it is not that same audience of decision makers who read

Time and *Newsweek,* which are primarily news media.

Time and *Newsweek,* besides spawning such notable imitations as *Der Spiegel* in West Germany and *L'Express* in France, have been quite successful as transnational publications, and both can claim strong appeal to that internationally minded readership. *Time,* over the years, has evolved into a multinational news medium for a multinational audience. *Time's* total circulation was 6.05 million in 1986. Of that, *Time Canada's* share was 340,831; *Time Europe's* (including Africa and the Middle East), 531,239; the edition for the Pacific region, 368,110; and for Latin America, 90,744.[7] So a good share of *Time's* copies were read abroad. Readership studies found that *Time's* readers abroad are affluent, multilingual, and cosmopolitan, often including a comparatively young business executive who is "likely to be internationally oriented in his economic and political opinions."[8] *Time* has increasingly tailored the editorial contents of its regional edition to those readers' interests, and for advertisers abroad, the magazine has offered more than sixty different editions based on geography.

Newsweek, with a foreign readership of over 872,000 out of its total 1986 circulation of 3,059,410, has done much the same thing overseas. *Newsweek International* has carried hundreds of exclusive stories and featured numerous covers, all different from the domestic edition. While *Time* tailored its overseas editions to regional interests, *Newsweek* tried to be more global in its approach. Only about 15 percent of its readers abroad are Americans; the rest are from 150 countries. *Newsweek* has always has signed columns, but American columnists rarely appear in the international edition. Instead, the magazine publishes another team of internationalists who include journalists from Australia, Italy, Britain, Indonesia, West Germany, France, Japan, and Sri Lanka.

Another American competitor of the news magazines abroad is the *Wall Street Journal.* With a satellite-assisted leap across the Pacific, the highly successful *Journal* launched in 1976 an Asian edition in Hong Kong that covers a sixteen-country, 6,000-square-mile business beat from Manila to Karachi. Averaging twelve pages, one-third the size of the domestic edition, the *Asian Wall Street Journal* tries for the same mix of authoritative business and political news, a risky experiment for a region with so little press freedom.

And pressures have been applied. In November 1985, the editor of the *Asian Wall Street Journal* apologized to a Singapore court for any contempt of court raised by a *Journal* editorial commenting on Singapore politics. The incident raised issues about the appropriate responses when a foreign court challenges the editorial freedom of an American newspaper published abroad.[9] And in February 1987, as a result of a story on a Singapore stock exchange, the *Journal*'s circulation was reduced from 5,000 to 400 copies by the government.

No such problems have risen as yet in Hong Kong, which, after Japan, enjoys the most press freedom in Asia. As such, Hong Kong has become the major news center in the region and home for a large contingent of foreign correspondents as well as the publishing center for the *Far Eastern Economic Review, Asiaweek, Newsweek, IHT,* and *Asian Wall Street Journal.* However, this open situation may end when the Crown Colony comes under the political control of China in 1997.

The *Journal*'s Asian enterprise is only possible because of space-age technology. With a small Asian-based staff of writers and editors, the paper relies on the resources of its domestic organization. The *Journal* transmits daily more than a 40,000-word file of stories and headlines from New York to Hong Kong in less than an hour. This material is re-edited and then printed in time to make the midday airline flights to other Asian capitals. The copy from New York is sent at 1,000 words a minute via high-speed computers using satellite circuits, then is converted from computer tapes directly into paste-up columns for photo-offset.

In 1983, the *Wall Street Journal* launched its European edition, printed in Heerlen, the Netherlands, and written and edited in Brussels, Belgium. The paper, which can be purchased on the day of publication throughout Europe and Britain, is edited for the international business executive working in Europe.[10]

Almost anywhere one travels abroad, stacks of foreign publications can be found on newsstands, especially in Third World countries. An American tourist in Paris has a choice of the *IHT, Time, Newsweek, USA Today,* or *Wall Street Journal.* A traveler arriving in francophone Abidjan, the capital of Ivory Coast, is impressed to find almost all the major French magazines plus that day's editions of the Paris dailies, all flown in by jet. Similarly, in Nairobi, Kenya, a choice of British papers, including same-day delivery of the Sunday papers, is available at hotels and newsstands. This plentitude of reading matter may represent unfair competition with the struggling local press, but these publications do provide a window on the world for that small but essential group of influentials who want to be informed about world affairs.

Changes in News Services

The subtle changes in the world news services as they have expanded in postwar years are further evidence of this growing internationalization of transnational media. Although they claim to "cover the world," the agencies historically have tended to serve primarily their own national clients and those in their spheres of influence; that is, Reuters serviced British media and the British commonwealth, AFP, the French press and overseas French territories, and UPI long had strong connections in Latin America. But these world agencies have become more international in scope, selling their services to whoever will buy wherever they may be. UPI, for example, had a French-language service that competed with AFP for provincial French newspapers and for clients in francophone Africa; the agency still operates its Spanish-language service. AFP is now used in many countries of the British Commonwealth. AP is so widely used in Germany that it is practically a German service and a strong competitor to Deutsche Press Agentur (DPA).

In addition, the personnel of world agencies have become significantly internationalized. Formerly, the AP, for example, boasted that its news from abroad was reported by American AP correspondents who had experience in running an AP bureau in the United States. The agency would not depend on foreign nationals to provide news from their own countries for AP use in the United States.

That has changed. With the increased professionalism of journalists abroad, news agencies not only find it more economical to use qualified local journalists but often get better reporting from whose who know their own country, its language, and its social and political traditions. Today, of 400 AP staffers abroad, only 100 are Americans. Three of AP's five Pulitzer Prizes for Vietnam War reporting went to Peter Arnett, a New Zealander; Horst Fass, a German; and Huynh Cong Ut, a Vietnamese. UPI maintained a multinational staff overseas that included two senior executives with British and French citizenship.

Nevertheless, ties to their own national media clients remain strong (no overseas client can be a member of the AP cooperative), and the news values of these domestic clients are of major importance in deciding news priorities, even though it makes sense for a world news agency to sell its services overseas as widely as possible. For example, the more customers there are in Latin America for UPI, the easier it is for UPI to collect Latin American news, and, in turn, the greater the incentive not only to send that news to American clients but also to distribute it among Latin American clients.

Although the world news agencies are accused of neocolonial domination of news flow to and from the Third World, the fact remains that these highly competitive services must *sell* their news reports, and to make them saleable or useful to editors and broadcasters abroad, a news agency must supply news that foreign editors are interested in using. Furthermore, in many Third World nations, world news agency reports are sold directly to national or official news agencies, which redistribute them to local media.

For notwithstanding the expansion of the world agencies since 1945, some 120 national and regional news agencies now operate, mostly in the newly independent nations of the Third World. Usually official or government controlled, they function mainly to collect and disseminate news within their own boundaries for their own media and to exchange news with the world news agencies. The Ghana News Agency, for example, supplies news about Ghana to Reuters, which has no correspondent in Ghana, and Reuters, in turn, sends the Reuters' Africa Service to the Ghana News Agency for redistribution to local media.

Numerous efforts have been made in recent years to organize these national agencies into continental or regional services to compete effectively with the world agencies. These efforts are discussed in Chapter 8.

Another facet of internationalization is foreign syndication of news by major daily papers. The New York Times News Service sends over 50,000 words daily to 550 clients of which over 130 are newspapers abroad. Its close competitor is the Los Angeles Times–Washington Post News Service, which transmits about 60,000 words daily to about 600 newspapers, half of which are outside the United States. This total includes papers in West Germany and elsewhere that receive the DPA with which the service is affiliated.

Some major European papers also sell their news and features abroad. Subscribers to this supplemental news are generally the larger and more prestigious papers, mostly in Western nations, which use the material to supplement other sources.

As noted previously, there is syndication also of television news film and videotapes, especially those of America's NBC, CBS, and ABC and Britain's BBC, most of it distributed by two Anglo-American firms—Visnews and WTN—via videotape and satellite to almost every television service in the world. Probably more international cooperation than competition exists in the transnational video film business because most nations have only one government-controlled television service. Jeremy Tunstall has described the Visnews operation:

> In addition to its core of BBC, NBC, and NHK (Japan) news-film, Visnews has its own staff of television reporters and stringers around the world. On any day it has about 30 video stories of which some 8 or 10 are sent to any individual television client. At Visnews headquarters in west London not far from Heathrow Airport, it is possible to see set out on just two sheets of paper a table indicating which of today's video stories are going to which of the 193 customers in 98 countries and territories of the world. Of the 12 or 15 minutes sent each day to each client, the typical television network used 4 or 5 minutes each day on its news bulletins, whilst some poorer television networks used the full 12 to 15 minutes day after day.[11]

Unlike the print media, which usually carry a credit line on agency reports or syndicated material, syndicated television news is usually presented anonymously. Whether watching in New Orleans or Nairobi, the viewer is rarely told who supplied the foreign video news. Therefore, most viewers around the world are unaware that Visnews and WTN dominate the distribution so completely.

Advertising, too, has followed the global trend. Recent "mega-mergers" among advertising and marketing services companies point up how internationalized Madison Avenue, the symbolic home of advertising, has become.

In May 1986, the biggest merger in advertising history took place when Saatchi & Saatchi of London agreed to buy Ted Bates Worldwide for $450 million. Saatchi & Saatchi thus became the world's largest agency, with U.S. billings for 1985 of $4.6 billion and world billings of $7.6 billion. Soon thereafter, the second largest advertising empire was created with the amalgamation of three other major concerns—Doyle Dane Bernbach Group, BBDO International, and Needham Harper Worldwide—which combined had in 1985 world billings of $5 billion and U.S. billings of $3.7 billion.[12]

Agency executives involved in the merger cited the industry's understanding of the need to offer clients worldwide service as a primary motivation. As an executive of Young & Rubicam pointed out: "There is a trend toward global assignment of agencies. If you don't have a complete set of worldwide resources, you're in danger of being left out in terms of getting the best clients."[13]

Increased communication, as was stressed earlier, leads to increased organization and consequently some concentration of control in the international news media. Fewer and fewer editors and broadcast executives are making editorial decisions for more and more people. The need to cooperate and join together in organizations seems at times stronger than the demands of independence and competition. Regional and continental media organizations are playing increasingly crucial roles in international news communication.

A prime example of such supranational cooperation is the European Broadcasting Union (EBU), which has developed some highly regarded news exchanges on Eurovision. London is a major television news center, in part, because it has the advantage of membership in the Eurovision News Exchange (EVN).

The first proposals for the EVN were made in 1957, and after limited experience in 1958–59 among eight countries, a daily exchange began in 1960.[14] This unusual example of international journalistic cooperation extends from Western to Eastern Europe, North and South America, North Africa, and the Middle East. The EVN affords rapid access to news stories produced daily by the national television services and news film agencies of the twenty-two countries of Western Europe, North Africa, and the Middle East, which are full members of the EBU.

Charles Sherman, who studied the EVN operation, wrote:

The EVN is an outstanding example of international pragmatism and cooperation. It illustrates how professional news and interests can readily unite diverse cultures and personalities in joint action. While the EVN may serve some altruistic purposes, it was only established to provide members with a rapid and efficient means of transporting highly perishable news items. It can deliver its cargo almost instantly from one country to another without being delayed by customs, bad weather, or other obstacles faced by systems which physically transport newsfilm.[15]

Similar organizational feats have been achieved by the International Radio and Television Organization headquartered in Prague and serving the Intervision network of East European television outlets. Although their activities and purposes vary greatly, the roster of international broadcasting organizations is impressive: the Union of National Radio and Television Organizations of Africa, the Asian Broadcasting Union, the Inter-American Association of Broadcasters, the Commonwealth Broadcasting Conference, and the International Telecommunications Union. Among print organizations, the International Press Institute and the Inter American Press Association are the most important of the non-Communist, nongovernmental organizations. The IPI and IAPA enable independent newspapers to respond in a coordinated and often effective way to international threats to freedom of the press.

The main point of all this is that the news media of individual nations, working through international organizations, are going through subtle institutional changes even though considerable provincialism, touched by nationalistic concerns, still permeates their activities. Much of the activity of these international media organizations does concern broader transnational purposes, and that is important.

English as Media Language

Effective communication across national borders naturally requires that sender and receiver communicate in a mutually understandable language. More and more that language is English, which is clearly the leading tongue of international communication today. Among the "Big Ten" of world languages in

1985, English ranked second with 415 million speakers after Mandarin Chinese with 771 million and is ahead of Russian with 282 million speakers, Spanish with 285 million, Arabic with 171 million, and German with 118 million. Furthermore, English is more widely used geographically, and for many millions of educated persons around the world it is their second language. In Europe, English is the most popular second language among younger people. An estimated 600 million speak it either as a primary or secondary language and can therefore be "reached" through English. Furthermore, this number includes most of the world's leaders. Unquestionably, English has become *the* global language of science and technology, with half the scientific literature of the world and most computer programs written in English. For many Third World nationals, English is the language of education, providing an entree to knowledge and information. (But one unfortunate result is that many native English speakers, especially Americans, have much less incentive than, say, Israelis, Dutch, or Swedes to learn other peoples' languages. Few Americans even learn to speak Spanish, although it is widely spoken here and is the first language of over 90 percent of our more than 20 million Hispanic population.)

For these and other reasons, English has also become the leading media language in international communication. Most of the world's news — whether by cable, shortwave radio, telex, telegraph, or comsats — is carried in English. Not only AP, UPI, Reuters, and Visnews but also AFP, DPA, and even TASS transmit some of their news in English, as do many national news agencies.

Moreover, English is the leading linguistic medium in a major field of world communication: shortwave radio broadcasting targeted to audiences in foreign countries.[16] A total of 100 broadcasting outlets with central studios in eighty-four countries use English as a means of reaching listeners beyond their national frontiers. The Soviet Union, China, East Germany, Japan, the Philippines, and Sri Lanka use English in some of their foreign broadcasts.

The imperialism of nineteenth-century Britain was a major reason, of course, why so many people from Singapore to India to Kenya to Nigeria to Bermuda converse today in English. Not unrelated is the phenomenon of the many English-language daily newspapers flourishing today in countries where English is neither the official nor even the most widely used language. Beginning with the

Chronicle of Gibraltar in 1801, English-language dailies, catering to expatriates, the foreign community, and local educated elites, have long survived, if not always flourished, in such diverse metropolises as Mexico City, Caracas, Paris, Rome, Athens, Cairo, Beirut, Manila, Bangkok, Singapore, and Tokyo as well as throughout India and Pakistan and the former British territories of Africa such as Nigeria, Ghana, Sierra Leone, Uganda, Kenya, Tanzania, Zimbabwe, and Zambia. In parts of polyglot Africa, English has almost evolved into another African language because of the role it plays in education, commerce, and mass communication.

Most of the artifacts of mass culture that move across national borders are in English. Tunstall said that English is the language best suited for "comic strips, headlines, riveting first sentences, photo captions, dubbing, sub-titling, pop songs, billboards, disc-jockey banter, news flashes, sung commercials."[17]

English, the most widely spoken language of Western Europe, is fast gaining currency in the Communist countries of Eastern Europe. In Poland and Czechoslovakia, words like "trip," "smoke," "car," "dance," "gag," and dozens of others are part of young people's vocabulary. "English for You" is one of the most widely followed language courses on East German television, and English courses at evening schools are invariably overfilled.

Young East Germans, Czechs, and Hungarians, like the earlier postwar generation of West Europeans, tend to pick up their vernacular English from English-language broadcasts on Radio Luxembourg and the American Armed Forces Network. They avidly memorize the texts of popular songs, a method the BBC has adopted for one of its language courses beamed abroad. For the East European, as for the West African or the South Asian, English becomes essential for links to the outside world.

This thrust of English as a world media language has become self-generating, and any educated person of whatever nationality who wishes to participate in our shrinking and interdependent world finds it useful to know English. In fact, since English is now spoken by more nonnative speakers of English than the British and the Americans combined, it must now be considered as belonging to the world, as indeed it does. For when two persons of differing linguistic backgrounds are able to converse, the chances are they will be speaking English.

The English language has been described as the greatest neocolonialist force in the world today. Perhaps in some contexts it is, but more important, English is the principal language in which the world communicates with itself.

NOTES

1. "International Herald Tribune Begins Singapore Satellite Edition," *Editor & Publisher,* Oct. 9, 1982, p. 28.
2. William Read, *America's Mass Media Merchants* (Baltimore: Johns Hopkins University Press, 1976), p. 14.
3. Ibid., p. 15.
4. Ibid.
5. Edwin McDowell, "Why the Digest Finally Wants to Make Money," *New York Times,* Feb. 9, 1986, section 3, p. 6.
6. Read, *America's Mass Media Merchants,* p. 136.
7. *1986 IMS Directory of Publications* (Ft. Washington, Pa.: IMS Press, 1986), pp. 727–28.
8. Read, *America's Mass Media Merchants,* p. 124.
9. Alex Jones, "Journal's Apology Troubles the Press," *International Herald Tribune,* Nov. 30, 1985, p. 1.
10. "Despite Glitches, the First European Wall Street Journal Gets Out on Time," *Editor & Publisher,* Feb. 12, 1983, p. 31.
11. Jeremy Tunstall, *The Media Are American: Anglo-American Media in the World* (London: Constable, 1977), p. 36.
12. Richard W. Stevenson, "Ad Agency Mergers Changing the Business," *New York Times,* May 13, 1986, p. 1.
13. Ibid.
14. Charles E. Sherman and John Ruby, "The Eurovision News Exchange," *Journalism Quarterly* 51, no. 3 (Autumn 1974):478.
15. Ibid., p. 485.
16. Donald R. Browne, *International Radio Broadcasting* (New York: Praeger, 1982), p. 4.
17. Tunstall, *Media are American,* p. 128.

6
Polishing the Prism: Public Diplomacy and Propaganda

> Propaganda and Censorship are the Twin Arms of Political Warfare. . . . The report of an event is as important as the event itself. . . . Propaganda only spreads the germs, it is the organization that maintains the epidemic.
>
> —*maxims on propaganda*

O
N any given evening, an Arab riding a camel at night in the desert outside of Khartoum, a Peruvian llama herder in a shelter in the Andes, or a Dane at home in Copenhagen can share a common communication experience. By merely flicking on a shortwave radio receiver and twisting the dials, each will hear the same polyglot cacophony of sounds detailing the news, unfolding diverse feature programs, and playing all sorts of music. The variety of languages spoken is immense, but each listener can, with little difficulty, find a program he or she understands.

Nowhere is the prism of international communication more apparent. In shortwave broadcasting, one person's "truth" or news is another's "propaganda." And vice versa. Transnational radio is perhaps the prime conveyor of what is sometimes called "public diplomacy."

Much of the flood of messages constantly washing over the globe is not neutral or disinterested information but purposive communication—words, sounds, and images intended to have an effect and to influence attitudes and opinions. A great deal of what refracts through the prism of international radio is purposive and is often called "propaganda," that is, the systematic use of words or symbols to influence the attitudes or behaviors of others. Propaganda is a loaded term, a pejorative epithet subjectively defined as a "persuasive statement I don't like." No one—journalist, broadcaster, writer, or educator—wants to be called a propagandist. Transnational communicators put on their ideological blinders and insist, "*We* deal in information or truth. *They* deal in propaganda."

"International political communication" (IPC), cumbersome though it is, is a useful and neutral expression encompassing such terms as public diplomacy, overseas information programs, cultural exchanges, and even propaganda activities and political warfare. A useful definition of IPC is: the political effects that newspapers, broadcasting, films, exchanges of persons, cultural exchanges, and other means of international communication can achieve.

However, a distinction should be made between international communication messages designed to have a political effect and those not, as well as between official and private communication. Here, then, are four broad categories of IPC:[1]

1. Official communication *intended* to influence foreign audiences (i.e., public diplomacy), such as those by the U.S. Information Agency (USIA), Voice of America (VOA), Radio Moscow, TASS, British Information Service, Deutsche Welle, Radio Havana, World Service of the British Broadcasting Corporation. Most international broadcasting falls in this category, and almost every nation with the capability will sponsor some broadcasting efforts across its borders.

2. Official communication *not intended* to influence foreign audiences, a small category indeed. One example is the U.S. Armed Forces Radio and Television network. At its peak, AFN operated some 200 radio and thirty TV transmitters serving American forces overseas and in the process acquired a huge "evesdropping" audience. Many young Europeans developed a taste for American music and learned to speak American English by listening to AFN.

3. Private communication *intended* to politically influence foreign audiences. This is another small category including various organizations and groups working to promote international under-

standing, for example, peace groups advocating a freeze on nuclear weapons. "Crossroads Africa," a private group operating with U.S. funds, possibly qualifies.

Sometimes, however, seemingly private groups are covertly financed by governments, such as the International Organization of Journalists headquartered in Prague, ostensibly a nongovernment journalists' organization, but one clearly controlled by Moscow. For years, Radio Free Europe in Munich was apparently supported by private contributions, although it later became known that the CIA provided most of its funds.

4. Private communication *without a political purpose.* Among these would be Western news agencies, media enterprises overseas such as advertising agencies, and distributors of motion pictures and television programs. Activities of church groups and medical missionaries belong in this classification as well. The great flow of American mass culture (much of it movies, music videos and pop recordings, and television programs produced within a five-square-mile area of Hollywood) has both negative and positive influences on international political communication. Without doubt, the impact of private U.S. mass communication overseas is far greater than that of U.S. public diplomacy through USIA and VOA.

Lines between these four categories often become blurred. This writer was puzzled, for instance, to find U.S. paperback books selling far below U.S. prices in African bookstores. Later, he learned the U.S. government covertly subsidized the sale of these paperbacks. Whether or not this is propaganda, even if the books are of clear educational value, is an arguable point. Often newsreels and short features are shown in African movie theaters without being identified as a free service of the French or British government. Much of the popular music heard on private radio stations in Latin America is provided by VOA.

Official IPC efforts are usually a supplement to diplomacy — ways by which governments try to extend their influence abroad and pursue their foreign policy objectives. The Western approach to public diplomacy, as conducted by the United States, Britain, France, and West Germany, is quite different from that of the Soviet Union and other Communist nations.

The international news media of both systems play a role in international political communication. The privately owned media organizations of the West serve their own commercial purposes of distributing and selling news and entertainment around the globe without intentional political aims. Yet the Western media transmit a good deal of purposive government information because all governments work hard at getting *their* versions of news and events into the world's news media. The media serve the purposes of public diplomacy whether they carry a story of President Reagan's denunciations of terrorism or one of Colonel Gaddafi's denials of any collaboration with terrorists. A continuing problem for the professional journalist is that of separating legitimate news from self-serving official "interpretations" of the news—whatever the source. Nevertheless, the two are often identical.

The Communist news media, by their own definition (see Communist press concept in Chap. 2), serve as unquestioning conduits of political communication from their own governments. Editors of TASS or *Pravda* face no professional dilemmas over whether or not to carry stories supporting Soviet foreign policy interests. This may be true as well in authoritarian governments where crucial news judgments are often made by government officials, not professional journalists.

Generally, Third World nations are on the receiving end of public diplomacy because most lack the communication capability to compete globally. A partial exception has been the extensive radio broadcasting by a few developing nations—the Voice of the Arabs station under Egypt's Abdul Gamal Nasser, for example. On the other hand, many Third World nations have benefited from the cultural exchanges and educational assistance from developed nations—all aspects of public diplomacy.

International Radio Broadcasting

In this day of direct broadcast satellites, global television, and other flashy new communications gadgetry, the powerful and pervasive medium of international radio broadcasting, long capable of carrying messages around the world almost instantaneously, is easily taken for granted. In the 1930s, political leaders such as Nazi Germany's Josef Goebbels talked of international radio as a "limitless medium" and saw it as a powerful instrument of international diplomacy, persuasion, and even coercion. And for over half a century, transnational radio has been just that — a key instrument of international political communication as well as many other things.[2]

The medium enjoyed a rapid and diverse expansion and by the late 1930s was being utilized by national governments, religious organizations, commercial advertisers, domestic broadcasters, and educators to carry their messages across national borders. The medium's growth and diversity continues today with the utilization of medium wave and FM as well as shortwave. Because most Americans, unlike many other peoples, do not listen much to international radio, they are unaware of how pervasive it is.

Anyone interested in making contact with the vast world of international radio can buy a small shortwave radio (less than $100) and a copy of the latest issue of *World Radio TV Handbook,* published in Denmark annually, which gives the program schedules and information on how to listen in on any of the over 3,800 shortwave stations scattered around the world. The activities of individual stations vary greatly. They offer from two or three to sixty or more language services broadcasting for 10 to 100 hours a day or more. The formats are equally diverse: newscasts, talks, interviews, editorial comments, press reviews, and documentaries. News coverage of domestic and foreign events is a key feature, but other informational programs try to reflect the broader cultural, social, and economic aspects of particular nations through dramas, music, sports events, and religious services.[3]

Here we are concerned with the largest international broadcasting operators. In order of total hours of weekly broadcasting, they are: the Soviet Union, the United States, the People's Republic of China, West Germany, Great Britain, North Korea, Albania, Egypt, India, Cuba, East Germany, Australia, the Netherlands, Japan.

The loudest voices in world broadcasting — Radio Moscow, Radio Beijing, VOA, Deutsche Welle and Deutschland Funk, BBC World Service, and Radio Cairo — rely mainly on the following languages, in descending order of usage: English, Russian, Mandarin Chinese, Arabic, Spanish, French, Japanese, Indonesian, Portuguese, German, Italian, Persian (Farsi), Swahili, Hindi, Hausa, and Korean.[4]

A significant portion of international political rivalries and

frictions are refracted through the prism of international broadcasting—the stresses between the Soviet Union and the United
States, the Arab/Israeli tensions, the North/South disputes between rich and poor nations, plus dozens of smaller regional controversies between nations.

Radio Moscow and its related Soviet broadcasters are on the
air over 2,000 hours a week, spending an estimated $700 million
annually to get Moscow's version of events to the world.[5] Radio
Moscow has nearly twice as many transmitters as VOA, broadcasting twenty-four hours a day to Europe and twenty-one hours a day
to America.[6] The United States counters with sixteen hours daily of
Russian-language VOA broadcasts into the Soviet Union, while
U.S.-backed Radio Free Europe broadcasts into Eastern Europe
and Radio Liberty to various parts of the Soviet Union.

Amid the cacophony of sometimes strident and pejorative
voices clashing over the international airwaves, it is important to
remember that international radio is a substantial news source for
many millions. But nowhere is the truism that one person's news is
another's propaganda more apparent. Listeners range the dials to
find a version of world events that suits their own needs and world
views; this is especially true for people living under dictatorships
that lack popular support. News on international radio may often
be acrimonious and self-serving, but without question it provides a
diversity of news and views for many millions.

When a political crisis or attempted coup occurs in an African
nation, for example, local broadcasters usually go off the air; resi-
dents then tune to BBC World Service or VOA to find out what is
happening in their own country.

The first days after the Chernobyl nuclear accident during
April/May 1986 illustrated the role that international broadcasting
can, on occasion, play. With the Soviet government providing
scant information, Radio Free Europe (RFE) and Radio Liberty
became a source of breaking news to the Soviet bloc audience.
Their programs also stressed practical advice for survival. The Pol-
ish-language service of RFE was on the air two hours ahead of
Polish radio stations with the news that high radiation levels had
been detected in Scandinavia and with the subsequent Soviet an-
nouncement that the accident had indeed occurred. RFE repeatedly
broadcast an interview with a Polish-speaking hematologist in New
York who gave advice including how to wash possibly contaminated vegetables.

"Whenever there is a crisis, there is a craving for information and they go out of the cities and into rural areas where there is no jamming to get information," said one RFE official about Soviet radio listeners.[7]

VOA and BBC both focussed on the accident itself without providing precautions advice. According to Richard Carlson of VOA, the radio broadcasts were "a perfect example" of the "terribly important" role that VOA and other Western stations play in providing information to people in the Soviet bloc.[8]

Three weeks after the accident, the Polish government was still having credibility problems when trying to reassure its citizens that the radiation danger had subsided. To allay fears, it took the unusual step of rebroadcasting VOA reports that tests at the U.S. Embassy in Warsaw showed no dangerous levels of radiation. Afterward, a Polish commentator noted that VOA was telling the truth this time.[9]

Diversity of news or news that conflicts with the official version of events is not welcome in the Soviet Union, which spends more than $900 million a year to jam Russian-language broadcasts from the West, more than three times the total annual budgets of $260 million of VOA, Radio Liberty, and RFE combined.[10]

With so much self-serving propaganda filling the night air (when reception is best), the credibility of an international station's news and commentaries is crucial for its reputation among foreign listeners. The international broadcaster that has long enjoyed the best reputation for believability and objectivity is the World Service of the BBC. As a public corporation, the domestic BBC is financed by license fees paid by each British household with a radio or television set. In theory, the BCC is wholly independent of the government of the day, although BBC governors are appointed by the government and the home secretary has, in some extreme circumstances, the right to censor programs. In 1985, BBC's cherished independence was twice called into question. In one instance, M.I.5, the British security service, was alleged to have controlled the hiring and firing of BBC staffers; in another, the BBC board of governors banned a program about Northern Ireland after the home secretary forcefully and publicly called for its withdrawal.[11] (The program was later aired after some editing.)

BBC's high credibility abroad has developed because the World Service only broadcasts news and programming originally prepared for the domestic services of the BBC. The highly professional reporters and stringers, at home and abroad, are essentially reporting to British radio listeners, and from this input are selected (without intervention of the Foreign Office) the news and features for the World Service. This approach ensures that the World Service reflects the diversity of British public opinion and BBC professionalism and not necessarily the views of the current government. During Britain's war with Argentina over the Falkland Islands, Margaret Thatcher bitterly criticized the BBC for not sufficiently supporting the British war effort. Some saw this as evidence of BBC's independence, the independence that draws so many listeners to BBC during times of crisis. The World Service, funded by the British government at $160 million a year, broadcasts in thirty-seven languages and has an estimated ten million listeners in Eastern Europe and the Soviet Union. Two other organizations, the British Council, which deals with cultural affairs, and the British Information Services supplement the broadcasting service in Britain's efforts at public diplomacy.

U.S. Activities in Public Diplomacy

U.S. efforts in public diplomacy share many similarities with those of Britain, but there are some important differences. The USIA, peacetime successor of the Office of War Information, is the key agency, which works closely with but separately from the Department of State. VOA began broadcasting in 1942 and is under the aegis of USIA. VOA broadcasts over 800 hours weekly in forty-two languages.[12] An estimated 120 million people around the world listen to the Voice each day.

VOA's efforts are supplemented by RFE, which broadcasts 555 hours weekly to Eastern Europe, while Radio Liberty broadcasts 462 hours weekly in Russian and fourteen other languages to the Soviet Union but not in English.[13]

The USIA, operating in 1986 with a budget of $837 million, employed about 12,000 people between Washington and some 275 U.S. Information Service (USIS) posts in 110 countries. Typically, a USIS post works under a U.S. ambassador and includes a library. USIS personnel cooperate with local media by providing news and related material, holding exhibits, running language courses, giving seminars of various kinds, and arranging visits and cultural exchanges of both Americans and local people.

USIA and VOA have long had an identity crisis: are they objective news and cultural organizations reflecting the diversity of American life and culture or are they arms of the State Department, vigorously pushing U.S. foreign policy objectives? Past managerial participation of such well-known journalists as Edward R. Murrow, Carl Rowan, and John Chancellor suggests the former, but at other times, as during the Vietnam War and the Reagan administration, the latter role has been stressed. The original charge of USIA in 1952 was to "help achieve the U.S. foreign policy objectives by a) influencing public attitudes in other nations, b) advising the President, his representatives abroad, and various agencies and departments on the implications of foreign opinion for present and contemplated U.S. policies, programs and official statements."

The long-running dispute over VOA, the "government mouthpiece," vs. VOA, the "public radio," continually tests what VOA staffers know as the "charter" — Public Law 94-350, signed by President Ford in 1976, which was the result of years of feuding between VOA news editors and foreign service officers who wanted VOA controlled and censored.[14] It laid down three principles: (1) "VOA news will be accurate, objective, and comprehensive"; (2) VOA will "present a balanced and comprehensive projection of significant American thought and institutions"; (3) "VOA will present the policies of the United States clearly and effectively."

Some in VOA believe that its news credibility is diminished when it takes a stridently anti-Communist stance countering the "lies" and "distortions" of our adversaries. But others ask, Why engage in international radio unless you vigorously pursue our foreign policy goals? The schizophrenic nature of our public diplomacy activity is reflected in the various slogans that have appeared from time to time: "Tell the truth about America"; "Win the propaganda war"; "Reflect the diversity and pluralism of American life"; and "Win the hearts and minds of the Third World masses."

Another policy issue debated within the USIA concerns audience targeting, revolving on the question of who are we trying to influence. If it is the ruling elites of the world's nations, then the person-to-person efforts of USIS posts and various cultural and educational exchanges seem called for; if it is the mass publics, then expanded and more aggressive radio broadcasting seems appropriate.

Policy matters aside, there is no question that under President Reagan appointee Charles Wick as USIA director, the agency has reflected a tougher anti-Communist approach, especially in commentaries following VOA newscasts. Since 1981, the agency has undergone a transformation as thorough as any in its history, and this despite controversies involving Wick's somewhat simplistic views on public diplomacy.

Controversies included revelations that Wick compiled black lists of Americans considered too liberal to go abroad as USIA lecturers and that he illegally taped all phone calls to his office. An academic colleague of the author heard Wick tell an audience that the Fulbright program should be scuttled because "just a bunch of communists [from the U.S.] were being exchanged for other communists [from abroad]." The Fulbright program was not terminated and, in fact, has been expanded.

Under Wick, a close friend of Ronald Reagan, the agency has flourished with a budget that nearly doubled between 1981 and 1986. The agency undertook the development of a government television network, called Worldnet, with the potential of linking sixty overseas systems to USIA headquarters in Washington.

Worldnet has become what some USIA officials privately call "the jewel in the crown" of the administration's fascination with the aggressive propaganda activities that Ronald Reagan calls "telling the message of American democracy to the world."

One commentator called Worldnet "a major step in the evolution of a little-noticed aspect of President Reagan's approach to dealing with other countries. Over the past five years, the former actor who built a political reputation as 'the great communicator' has transformed the government's lackluster foreign information activities into the largest and most technologically adroit propaganda apparatus in the world."[15]

In addition to producing cultural and public affairs programs for local overseas networks, Worldnet has employed satellite links for two-way televised news conferences between foreign journalists and American public figures. Part of the programming in its first years included a two-hour program of news and features to Europe five days a week.[16]

A large portion of increased USIA funds has been spent to

improve VOA's equipment and technology. Under a $1.3 to $1.8 billion modernization program, VOA is expanding its broadcast reach and has signed agreements for new sites or improved existing sites in Morocco, Sri Lanka, Thailand, Costa Rica, and Belize. VOA planned to increase the number of languages broadcast from forty-two to sixty.

Another Reagan project was Radio Marti, a VOA-linked facility patterned after RFE, to broadcast news and commentary specifically to Cuba. Named for a Cuban independence hero and poet, the controversial station went on the air in May 1985, broadcasting news, entertainment, and sports in Spanish for fourteen and a half hours daily from studios in Washington, D.C., and a 50,000-watt AM transmitter in the Florida Keys. Opponents had argued that since Cubans regularly listen to U.S. radio and television stations, the new service was unnecessary. Further, they feared that Radio Marti might raise the level of anti-Castro propaganda, thereby worsening U.S.-Cuban relations. In the final legislation creating Radio Marti, Congress said it was intended to "serve as a consistently reliable and authoritative source of accurate, objective and comprehensive news."[17]

The public diplomacy efforts of Western nations such as the United States, Great Britain, France, and West Germany have much in common: similar broadcasting services stressing news, cultural exchanges, and the use of local information/cultural posts (usually including a library) in foreign capitals as a part of the diplomatic mission.

Communist Model of Public Diplomacy

Communist nations follow a somewhat different model, one more consistent with their ideology and political organization. Some observers believe that the Soviet Union is spending much more money and trying harder than the United States. (As with comparative estimates of military strength, the unadorned truth is hard to come by.) The CIA has estimated the the Soviet Union spends $3.3 billion annually on propaganda efforts. This includes such overt efforts as Radio Moscow and its related stations, which broadcast in eighty-two languages over

2,000 hours weekly at a cost of some $700 million, with $150 million also allocated for the Communist party's international activities.[18] The $550 million spent on TASS's indirect propaganda efforts of spreading Moscow's version of world events is also added to the estimated total. (The U.S. government does not subsidize AP and UPI, but these services obviously benefit U.S. information efforts.)

TASS provides most of the material for Radio Moscow, which has become over the years much more sophisticated in its efforts. Broadcasts now include Soviet-made jazz and rock music, and the broadcasts in English are particularly subtle, using announcers who apparently are hired for their ability to sound like VOA or BBC broadcasters. Other Moscow-aligned Communist countries deliver more than 5,000 hours a week of pro-Soviet (and mostly anti-U.S.) broadcasting a week, more than twice the output of Radio Moscow. (For comparison purposes, the broadcasting totals for BBC and Deutsche Welle should probably be added to the 1,800 weekly hours of VOA, RFE, and Radio Liberty.)

The Soviet state has traditionally made use of vigorous international communication; after all, the original movement under Marx and Lenin was an international one. Top Communist leaders have always taken an active part in public diplomacy efforts; it seems to go with the job. Nikita Khrushchev was good at personal public relations, and Mikhail Gorbachev has shown himself to be adept at winning friends abroad for Soviet policies. This top level concern, plus the totalitarian nature of the state, facilitates the adjustment of propaganda themes as national policies change or the international situation evolves. The Soviet Union successfully identified itself with the broad decolonization movement that created the Third World, making the world forget that the Soviet Union is itself the last great empire of disparate peoples on earth.

Soviet public diplomacy efforts are furthered by three groups in foreign lands. Foremost are the Moscow-aligned local Communist parties, which are organized to cooperate with Moscow, though their influence has declined in recent years. In addition, in 126 countries there are Soviet "friendship societies," which coordinate cultural exchanges, visits, and exhibitions. In 1979, a total of 53,300 students from the Third World were studying in the Soviet Union. In 1981, the Soviets offered 4,500 college scholarships in

Latin America, while the United States offered only 4 percent of that number.

Heavy reliance is placed as well on front groups and controlled organizations in other countries to help win influence. A good example is the International Organization of Journalists (IOJ), headquartered in Prague.

Another difference from the Western approach is the heavy use of direct mail to deliver all over the world vast numbers of books, pamphlets, and magazines, printed in many languages. A U.S. congressman, Toby Roth, said that each year the Soviets distribute 180,000,000 books and pamphlets around the world, while the U.S. distributes only about 200,000—less than 1 percent of the Soviet commitment.[19] (Under Wick, however, the number of American books put into foreign circulation was increasing by 200,000 a year.[20])

The Soviet "cold warrior," like his counterpart in the West, tries to utilize the local news media wherever possible. One often-used technique is to plant a specially prepared article in a foreign newspaper or magazine, then quote it back to the Soviet Union or other countries as a viewpoint current in the country of the article's publication.

The Soviet Union and the United States are not the only nations, of course, that participate in various forms of international political communication. Almost every nation that is able to maintain diplomatic representation abroad plays the game to some extent.

Polluting News Channels: Disinformation and Dirty Tricks

As we have seen, public diplomacy covers a wide variety of activities, but one aspect of particular importance for transnational news flow concerns the endeavors of intelligence organizations such as the KGB and the CIA to subvert or use the press and other media for their own purposes. Terms like "disinformation," "dirty tricks," and "co-opting journalists" are often used to describe these practices. In some respects, these efforts reflect the dilemma over how to be a great power in an immoral and untidy world. As one U.S. diplomat said, "We must be able to do something between lodging a diplomatic protest and sending in the Marines."

Although the discussion here concerns the Soviet Union and the United States, other nations, big and small, are not above trying to manipulate or pollute the world's news channels.

"Disinformation" refers to untrue or distorted material deliberately fabricated to mislead and is a major activity of the KGB; reportedly some 15,000 people in Moscow are involved in such efforts. On October 9, 1981, the U.S. State Department issued a four-page special report accusing the Soviet Union of using forgery, disinformation, and blackmail to discredit and weaken the United States and other nations. The report said, "The approaches used by Moscow include control of the press in foreign countries, outright and partial forgery of documents, use of rumors, insinuations, altered facts and lies, use of international front organizations, and the exploitation of a nation's academic, economic and media figures as collaborators to influence policies of a nation."[21]

In recent years, a good deal of such skulduggery has found its way into international news channels. The State Department report said that in one developing nation the Russians used more than two dozen local journalists to plant news items favorable to the Soviet Union. The report also stated that the Indian magazine *Blitz* disseminated Soviet-inspired documents and had been used to publish forgeries, falsely accusing Americans of being espionage agents in India.

In another nation, Moscow was accused of using local journalists to exercise substantial control over the contents of two major daily newspapers. In 1984, the largest daily newspaper in Greece, *Ethnos,* was accused of having links with the disinformation department of the KGB, and the publisher, George Bobolas, was said to be an "agent of influence" for the Soviet Union.[22]

Other disinformation examples cited in U.S. reports were aimed at the United States: the United States was accused of being behind the seizure of the Great Mosque in Mecca in 1979; the United States was blamed for the death of President Aldo Moro in Italy as well as the death in a plane crash of General Omar Torrijos, leader of Panama; in black Africa, the United States was accused of supplying arms to South Africa.

The effectiveness of these disinformation activities is difficult to assess, but experts speculate that because the Soviets spend so much money and effort on it, their leaders must think it pays dividends. As a former CIA official has pointed out, Soviet disinformation is circulated only by non-American news organizations, primarily in the Third World. An effective forgery operation, he said, requires a gullible audience, and the U.S. press and public are not fooled.[23]

However, Arnaud de Borchgrave, former *Newsweek* correspondent and editor of the *Washington Times,* strongly disagrees and believes that the U.S. news media have been compromised. In testimony before the House Intelligence Committee, he quoted former Czech disinformation official Ladislav Bittman's description of successful efforts to plant disinformation in U.S. and European newspapers. Claiming that a relatively high percentage of foreign agents are journalists, Bittman said, "A journalist operating in Britain, West Germany, or the U.S. is a great asset to Communist intelligence. There are many journalists who are agents. There are important newspapers around the world that have been penetrated by Communist intelligence services. A top secret KGB manual, entitled 'The Practice of Recruiting Americans in the U.S.A. and Third Countries,' listed in order of priority twelve categories of recruitment targets. The first was government personnel with access to classified information. The second was journalists."[24] Even more important, according to de Borchgrave, are the "unwitting dupes" who accept disinformation without challenging it. He described the two score defectors from East European intelligence services he had interviewed in recent years as astonished at the ease with which the KGB can conduct disinformation activities in the United States.

In October 1985, a VOA staff member told a conference at the Hoover Institute at Stanford that the KGB may have hundreds of recruited agents among foreign journalists, including some in the United States, "ready at any time to plant prepared stories in the national media." She attributed most of her information to two Russian defectors who had posed as journalists while working for the KGB.[25] In another report, a former KGB agent, who had worked as a TASS correspondent in Africa, said Moscow made elaborate efforts to plant disinformation articles in newspapers with both the witting and unwitting assistance of local journalists.[26]

Other Side of the Coin

Although even its critics concede that U.S. intelligence agencies make sparing use of false documents, Washington has a long history of covert efforts to influence press coverage and public opinion abroad. John Stockwell, a former CIA agent in Africa, charged in his book, *In Search of Enemies,* that articles were planted in 1975 and 1976 in both Angolan and Zambian newspapers recounting unsubstantiated U.S. allegations about Soviet involvement in Angola. More recently, a study sponsored by the Kennedy School of Government at Harvard disclosed that the State Department had in January 1978 drawn up plans for a covert action to sway European press coverage of the neutron bomb. The effort was said to involve "sympathizers and agents in the European press corps" who would work "either for money or for free." It is not known whether the plan was carried out.

In October 1986, the Reagan administration became involved in a controversy over reports that it had made selective disclosures of news and disinformation about Libya and its leader, Muammar Gaddafi. The *Washington Post* reported that the administration had devised a policy that included leaking to the U.S. press false information designed to convince Gaddafi that his country was about to be attacked by the United States or that he was about to be overthrown in a coup. The White House denied the existence of any plan to deceive the U.S. public, which, according to some press critics, only extended the disinformation. Administration officials, however, admitted that the White House had tried to disorient Gaddafi. U.S. news media leaders widely deplored any deliberate disinformation campaign as being unacceptable in a democratic society with a free press.

As the American Society of Newspaper Editors said in a telegram to President Reagan: "This calculated technique of falsehood, commonly employed by totalitarian governments as an instrument of policy, is repugnant to American democratic principles and destructive of the role of the press in a free society." Several weeks later, the State Department's official spokesman, Bernard Kalb, resigned as assistant secretary of state in protest of the disinformation activity.

The most complete picture of earlier CIA efforts to influence world opinion came out in 1977 in the report of the Senate Select Committee on Intelligence Activities, headed by Senator Frank Church. A three-part series in the *New York Times* that drew on the Church report revealed that the agency had channeled information and misinformation through a once-substantial network of newspapers, news agencies, and other communication entities, most of them based overseas, that it owned, subsidized, or otherwise influenced over the years. The CIA's propagandizing efforts, the *Times* reported, appear to have contributed to at least some distortions of the news at home as well as abroad. Here are the principal features of the "Mighty Wurlitzer," as it was dubbed:[27]

1. The CIA at various times owned or subsidized more than fifty newspapers, news services, radio stations, periodicals, and other communication entities, sometimes in the United States but mostly abroad, that were used as vehicles for its extensive propaganda efforts, as cover for its operations, or both. Another dozen foreign-based news organizations, while not financed by the CIA, were infiltrated by paid CIA agents.

2. Since the end of World War II, more than thirty and perhaps as many as 100 American journalists employed by a score of U.S. news organizations have worked as salaried intelligence operative, while performing their reportorial duties. A few worked for military intelligence and some worked for foreign intelligence services, including the KGB. (This represents, however, a small percentage of the hundreds of American journalists working overseas.)

3. Over the years at least eighteen American reporters have refused CIA offers, some ot them lucrative, to undertake clandestine intelligence operations.

4. Since 1945, at least a dozen full-time CIA agents have worked abroad as reporters or noneditorial employees of American news organizations, in some cases with the approval of the organization whose credentials they carried.

These activities raised serious ethical and other questions for the U.S. press, which has long valued its independence from government. Two major areas of concern were the potential for manipulating or misleading the American public and the damage to the credibility and independence of a free press.

As a result of these revelations, the CIA agreed to bar the paid use of journalists for secret intelligence operations except in extraordinary circumstances such as an "emergency involving human lives or critical national interests." In 1982, CIA Director William Casey reaffirmed this policy.[28]

The efforts by these and other intelligence organizations around the world to manipulate both news and news organizations are reminders of the central role that transnational news flow plays in today's world. All governments—big and small—do what they can to influence global news. And for the past decade, spokesmen for poor nations of the Third World have complained that the Western system of international news flow has either ignored or painted a badly distorted picture of the Third World.

NOTES

1. For some of these definitions and distinctions, I have relied on W. Phillips Davison, *International Political Communication* (New York: Praeger, 1965), pp. 9–10.
2. For a scholarly and authoritative study of this broad and complex subject, see Donald R. Browne, *International Radio Broadcasting* (New York: Praeger, 1982).
3. Ibid., p. 4.
4. Ibid., p. 359.
5. "The Propaganda Sweepstakes," *Time*, March 9, 1981, p. 34.
6. Peter Osterlund, "Voice of America Clears Throat," *Wisconsin State Journal*, Oct. 29, 1985, p. 8.
7. Alex S. Jones, "In a Crisis, Whom to Tune in, in the Soviet Bloc, Probably Western Radio," *New York Times*, May 3, 1986, p. 4.
8. Ibid.
9. Michael T. Kaufman, "Three Weeks Later, 'Cloud' still Bothers the Poles," *New York Times*, May 20, 1986, p. 7.
10. Jones, "In a Crisis."
11. R. W. Apple, "BBC Is Caught Up in New Furor," *New York Times*, Aug. 22, 1985, p. 3.
12. Browne, *International Radio*, p. 116.
13. Ibid., p. 358.
14. Robin Grey, "Inside the Voice of America," *Columbia Journalism Review*, May/June 1982, p. 25.
15. John M. Goshko, "Talk Not Cheap at Wick's USIA," *Washington Post*, March 31, 1986, p. A1.
16. Neil Lewis, "Wick Is Surviving the Criticism," *New York Times*, June 26, 1985, p. 12.

17. Joseph B. Treaster, "Radio Marti Begins Broadcasting," *New York Times,* May 21, 1985, p. 1.
18. "Propaganda Sweepstakes."
19. Frank Aukofer, "Ideals Can Be a Powerful Weapon, Says Roth," *Milwaukee Journal,* Oct. 4, 1981, p. 20
20. Goshko, "Talk Not Cheap."
21. Bernard Gwertzman, "U.S. Accuses Soviet of Disinformation," *New York Times,* Oct. 9, 1981, p. 3.
22. John Tagliabue, "Greek Editor Says the U.S. Is Trying to Intimidate His Paper," *New York Times,* May 20, 1984, p. 4.
23. Arnaud de Borchgrave, "Bum Tips and Spies," *New York Times,* Aug. 12, 1981, p. 21.
24. Ibid.
25. M. L. Stein, "The KGB and the Press," *Editor & Publisher,* Oct. 26, 1985, p. 11.
26. Stephen Engleberg, "A K.G.B. Defector Recalls Tactics of Informing to 'Disinform,' " *New York Times,* Feb. 11, 1986, p. 4.
27. John Crewdson and Joseph Treaster, "The CIA's 3-Decade Effort to Mold the World's Views," *New York Times,* Dec. 25, 26, 27, 1977, pp. 1ff.
28. Judith Miller, "C.I.A. on Using Journalists," *New York Times,* June 9, 1982, p. 8.

7

Challenges and Difficulties of Reporting World News

> The cause of the decline and fall of the Roman Empire lay in the fact that there were no newspapers of the day. Because there were no newspapers, there was no way by which the dwellers in the far-flung nation and the empire could find out what was going on at the center.
>
> *—H. G. Wells*

THE Nigerian press spokesman smiled at the roomful of reporters, paused dramatically, and said: "Gentlemen, I've got some good news for you today. We are lifting press censorship."

In the commotion that followed, one newsman was heard to shout: "Can we report that?"

"Unfortunately not," replied the spokesman. "You see, we never really said publicly that we were imposing press censorship. Therefore, we can hardly announce today that we are lifting it."[1]

Often when two or more foreign correspondents gather to relax, they exchange stories like this one that reflect the frustrations, the humor, and the ironies of what must be among the most demanding jobs in journalism. There is no question that transnational news gathering is an exacting occupation for the professional newsmen and women of Western nations who put together the various stories, reports, rumors, and educated guesses that make up the daily international news file. To them, theirs is a difficult, dangerous, and badly misunderstood enterprise. They understand its shortcomings and difficulties far better, they believe, than politically motivated critics. It is, they will point out, the only effective news-gathering system the world has; no viable alternatives exist or are likely to be developed soon.

In a real sense, the world's ability to learn the news about itself depends on what gets into the news flow in the fifteen or twenty open societies with highly developed media systems. Once an important story appears, for example, in New York, London, Paris, Rome, or Tokyo, it immediately starts flowing through the arteries of the world's news system and will be widely reported elsewhere — but not everywhere and certainly not every story. For the majority of non-Western governments act as gatekeepers, screening news in and out of their nations. These political controls, as well as poverty and illiteracy, deprive the great majority of the world's peoples from learning even the barest outline of major current events. But any major story that breaks in the West has the possibility of being reported throughout the world. Within hours after the explosion of the space shuttle *Challenger,* many millions worldwide heard the news and saw the dramatic pictures on their television screens.

To the few thousand foreign correspondents, the world's nations are strung out on a continuum from "free" or open at one end to "not free" or closed at the other. To illustrate, the Associated Press has little difficulty gathering news in open Sweden, since several newspapers there take AP services and share their own news and photos with the agency. In addition, AP correspondents can use other Swedish media as sources and can develop their own stories or easily gain access to public officials.

Sudan, as an example of a partly free country, offers a different kind of challenge. AP has no clients there, largely because the Sudan News Agency lacks the hard currency to buy the satellite-beamed AP world service. The local media are often subject to official controls, and the AP cannot economically justify maintaining a full-time correspondent in Khartoum. Therefore, AP covers Sudan by using a local stringer (a part-timer who is paid for what is used). Periodically, the AP may send in a staff correspondent to Sudan to do background or roundup stories.

At the "not-free" end of the continuum are a few countries that for years have barred all foreign journalists and news agencies. When something important happens in Tirana, Albania, for instance, AP and the world usually find out about it belatedly from a government-controlled Albanian radio broadcast monitored abroad or from travelers or diplomats coming out of the country. A foreign correspondent often defines a country as free or not free according to how much difficulty he or she has in reporting events from that country. This may sound narrow and self-serving, but it has validity; the freedom of access that a foreign reporter enjoys is usually directly related to the amount of independence and access enjoyed by local journalists themselves. If local journalists are harassed and/or controlled by a particular government, so very likely will be the foreign journalists.

Throughout the unstable Third World, some nations swing back and forth between freedom and controls. For example, under Indira Gandhi, India, the world's largest democracy, went through a not-free period when the local press was controlled and foreign correspondents were forced to leave or were subjected to censorship. Later, news access opened again and the country regained the free press for which India had been noted.

Despite the widespread availability of impressive gadgets and hardware — communications satellites, telex, video display terminals, computers — collecting news throughout the world is still an erratic and imperfect process. Some significant events are either not reported or reported long after the fact. Certain areas of the world, such as central Africa, rarely get into the world news flow. Datelines from such capitals as Niamey, Bamako, Khartoum, Ouagadougou, Lome, Freetown, Conakry, Bangui, Yaounde, Nouakchott, or Brazzaville seldom appear in Western newspapers unless the stories concern natural disasters, violent conflict, or a coup d'etat.

Central to this situation are disagreements between professional journalists and government officials over the nature of news. To the journalist, news is the first fragmentary and incomplete report of a significant event or happening that editors think will be of interest or importance to their readers or listeners. To many government officials, news is "positive" information that reflects well on their nation (and hence themselves) and serves their country's general interests and goals. Yet those same leaders want to know all that is happening elsewhere that affects their interests and country. Keith Fuller, former head of AP, put it well: "News is what a government official wants to read about somewhere else, propaganda is what the official wants the world to read about him and his country."

Politicians and government leaders in every nation from north to south attempt to manage or manipulate the news so that it favors their causes, their programs, their image.

Too Few Correspondents

"What is commonly referred to as the world flow of information," AP foreign correspondent Mort Rosenblum wrote, "is more a series of trickles and spurts. News is moved across borders by a surprisingly thin network of correspondents. . . . The smaller countries are squeezed into rapid trips during lulls between major stories in the larger countries." Rosenblum quoted a comment from a Latin American academic that "news breaks in South America along the direct line of the Braniff route."[2]

Considering the demand for foreign news and the difficulties of reporting it, there are probably far too few correspondents stationed overseas. Rising costs and inflation have made maintenance of a staffer overseas quite expensive. Estimates range from $125,000 to $200,000 for maintaining a bureau overseas for one year. The *New York Times* spends an average of $200,000 a year on each of its bureaus, or about $8,000,000 annually. Another $1,000,000 is spent on the *Times* foreign desk in New York. The *Baltimore Sun* (with only 170,000 circulation) maintains eight correspondents overseas at a cost of $1,000,000 annually. It is not surprising then, that so many news media rely on the news agencies for their foreign news.[3]

The number of American foreign correspondents seems to have stabilized in recent years. AP's foreign news corps grew from sixty-five full-time U.S. journalists in 1975 to 100 in 1985 but relies on some 300-plus foreign nationals to cover foreign news in its overseas bureaus.

In 1982, the *New York Times* had thirty-two full-time foreign correspondents, twenty-five part-timers, and twenty-three bureaus overseas. However, in 1968, the *Times* maintained forty-eight full-time correspondents overseas. The *Los Angeles Times* has been expanding its foreign coverage in recent years and in January 1986 opened a new bureau in Manila, bringing to twenty-four its number of foreign bureaus manned by staff correspondents. The *Washington Post* has also increased its staff of foreign reporters, which stood at seventeen in 1982.

Other print media with significant foreign staffs were the *Wall Street Journal* with a dozen reporters, *Time* magazine with thirty-five in twenty-two locations, *Newsweek* with twenty-one, *Christian Science Monitor* with eight, and the *Chicago Tribune* with five.[4]

The three major U.S. television networks have decided to leave vast areas of the world uncovered, in part, because of financial considerations. It has been estimated that it costs $1,000,000 a year to maintain even one "shoestring" bureau overseas. ABC has twenty-two reporters in thirteen locations abroad, CBS has a similar number in thirteen cities, and NBC has seventeen correspondents in thirteen cities.[5] Increasingly, the networks seem to be relying on news film supplied by the syndicates Visnews and WTN and other broadcasters for foreign coverage.

Not only are foreign correspondents comparatively few in number, they are unevenly distributed as well. Ralph Kliesch found that 54 percent of American reporters and 51 percent of all correspondents abroad were stationed in nineteen European countries. Of these, only 7 to 8 percent were in three East European nations, mainly the Soviet Union.[6]

The vast expanse of Africa, with over 500,000,000 people in forty-five countries, is very thinly covered by a declining number of Western journalists. However, when a major international story breaks, almost a herd instinct seems to stampede numerous reporters and cameramen and women to the scene. In 1986, about 170 accredited foreign correspondents were based in Johannesburg, due to the continuing racial unrest and because it was a hub for air travel and comsat transmission for southern Africa, where news was breaking not only in South Africa itself but in neighboring Zimbabwe, Namibia, Angola, and Mozambique as well. The 1983 civil war in Chad brought the largest number of journalists ever to gather in that impoverished former French colony. The Ministry of Information at N'Djamena, the capital, accredited 150 reporters, photographers, and television technicians from all over the world at the height of the Libyan intervention.[7] A few weeks later, almost all had departed.

During the height of the Iranian crisis when fifty-three Americans were held hostage, more than 300 Western newsmen and women, some 100 of them Americans, were working in Tehran. Such "parachute journalism" does not always provide informed coverage, because many of these reporters have had no previous experience in the country about which they are reporting.

New York and Washington, D.C., are major world news centers, drawing reporters from over seventy countries but principally from Britain, West Germany, Japan, France, Italy, and Canada. According to the USIA Foreign Press Center, 480 foreign correspondents were working in Washington in 1983.[8]

Such statistics reflect the reality that most world news originates in such major news "hubs" as New York, Washington, D.C., London, Paris, Tokyo, Hong Kong, Bonn, Rome, and Moscow, and foreign correspondents, by and large, tend to congregate in cities where news is either made or flows into.

For American readers, at least, serious questions have been raised about the quantity and quality of the foreign news they receive. The discussion tends to be circular. AP and United Press International editors have long maintained that their services gather ample amounts of foreign news but that their newspaper and broadcast clients do not use very much of it. The clients, in turn, say that their readers and viewers are not that interested in foreign news. Yet critics say that Americans are uninformed about the world because their news media report so little about it.

In one study of sixty daily newspapers in nine countries, the U.S. press ranked last in the percentage of total space (excluding advertising) devoted to foreign news. The data showed that U.S. newspapers devoted less than one-half (11.1 percent) the space to foreign news than did the sample papers of Western Europe (23.6 percent) and the nonaligned countries (22.8 percent) and less than one-third the space than the East European papers (37.5 percent) studied.[9] Yet the news hole is larger in most U.S. papers and more foreign news may be carried.

Certainly there is substance to the generalization that the majority of Americans, with access to the world's most pervasive media, are ill informed on world affairs. Foreigners traveling in the American heartland are uniformly impressed by the lack of world news in local media and the ignorance shown by most Americans about the outside world. By contrast, the average West German,

Dane, Swiss, or Israeli knows more global news because his or her media carry more.

Part of the problem is that Americans, like Russians and Chinese, have a continental outlook, living as they do in the midst of a vast land mass that encourages a self-centered, isolationist view of the world. With two friendly neighbors and protected by two oceans, Americans are slow to realize their interdependence with others.

Thus Americans' interest in foreign news has its ups and downs, depending on the immediacy of the impact on their lives of events abroad. During the Vietnam War, much concern was focused on happenings in Southeast Asia but not in Latin America or Africa. After Vietnam came a pulling back from foreign concerns as the nation became enthralled by Watergate and its aftermath. But after the rapid increases and then decreases in the price of foreign oil, the Soviet incursion into Afghanistan, continuing Arab/Israeli conflict, and the rising level of terrorism directed against Americans, the average American's interest (if not knowledge) in foreign news clearly increased.

Further, there is some evidence that the public is more interested in foreign news than editors believe. A Louis Harris poll on public attitudes toward news found that "those who work in the media (editors, news directors, and reporters) feel that only 5 percent of the public are greatly interested in international news. A much higher 41 percent of the public express deep interest in world affairs being covered in the news media."[10] A subsequent poll reinforced the evidence that Americans do care more about international matters. According to a February 1986 Gallup Poll, Americans cited international problems more than any others as the nation's most pressing concerns. Concerns listed included nuclear war, the arms race, and terrorism.[11]

Some scholars believe that television is profoundly affecting Americans' news perceptions. Professor Neil Postman believes television projects "a peek-a-boo" world, "where now this event, now that, pops into view for a moment, then vanishes again. It is a world without much sense or coherence. . . . Americans know of a lot of things but about almost nothing. Someone is considered well informed who simply knows that a plane was hijacked or that there was an earthquake in Mexico City."[12]

After the U.S. hostages in Tehran were freed in 1981, Postman conducted a study to determine the extent of knowledge about Iran. One hundred people were asked simple questions about the Iranian language, religion, and government. "Because Iran was carried almost continuously on the news for a year, we expected people would not only know about Iran but would be overloaded," Postman said. "But we found that most people couldn't answer our questions. Almost always those who actually knew something had gotten it from print sources."[13]

There is a growing recognition that perhaps the term "foreign news" is a misnomer, that in this interdependent world we are potentially affected by any event almost anywhere. American workers who lose jobs in manufacturing due to cheap foreign imports or farmers unable to sell wheat abroad due to the overvalued dollar are becoming more knowledgeable about world economic trends.

Robert Semple of the *New York Times* said, "Ask yourself, would the U.S. auto industry be in such bad shape if the Detroit papers had had men in Japan and Europe a decade ago? Would the U.S. steel industry be laying off workers if the Pittsburgh papers had been covering the European Economic Community and the Japanese steel industries and their export policies 10 years ago? People won't wake up to the importance of foreign news until a few more banks fail because of lousy foreign loans."[14]

Performance Criticized

The use of foreign news in the U.S. media raises two questions: Are news media fulfilling their obligation of providing essential information so their readers can make sound judgments on foreign and national affairs? Or are media contributing instead to making Americans more provincial at a time when the world is getting smaller?

A study based on a series of surveys of journalists and newspapers found that American newspapers generally are lax in their coverage of international news. Lester Markel and Audrey March concluded that the majority printed little more than the bare essentials, not enough to provide any clear view of what is going on in the rest of the world.[15]

The surveys determined that news space given to reporting of foreign news totaled 17 percent of the whole news allotment; however, this figure was misleading, the researchers pointed out, since it included trivia, features, and human interest stories, which if deducted would leave about 10 percent.

"As for quality, there is often a lack of expertness, due to the fact that correspondents are often shifted in order to get a fresh point of view and so do not have the feel of the country that a good dispatch reflects. Interpretation of international news is minimal and in some newspapers, nonexistent. Instead of interpretation, one is likely to find opinion in the guise of background."[16]

Furthermore, the evidence indicates that the press is not covering the Third World as well as it once did. Xan Smiley, a former correspondent for the *Times* of London, has suggested that journalists who reported crisis events in countries like Ghana and Tanzania in the early postindependence years soon found themselves in direct opposition to the governments of these nations and, with the threat of expulsion hanging over their heads, decided that only the major crisis events were worth reporting. Smiley has noted that heavy self-censorship is a standard feature of reporting by Western journalists throughout the Third World and that nowhere is it more rigorously observed than in Africa.[17]

Markel and March also undertook a week-long look at foreign news on the nightly television network news broadcasts. The amount of foreign news was found to be exceedingly low on all three networks; interpretation was virtually absent; objectivity, difficult to measure on brief stories, was rated adequate.

The indictment concludes:

> Critics of the newspapers and television news broadcasts charge that they fail to supply the essential facts accurately or in perspective; that they barrage the public with a welter of unrelated news stories; that they fail to separate the significant from the trivial; and, much too often, neglect the minority viewpoint. In general, the view was expressed that the media fail to show that international news is relevant to the lives of readers and viewers at a time when actions by the federal government and events in foreign countries may profoundly affect American lives.[18]

Michael J. Arlen, a perceptive television critic, believed that foreign news as a broadcast commodity has been in a steady decline to such an extent that "it now often seems to be thrown into a network's regular news productions as a kind of afterthought."[19] Even though CBS and NBC claim that the foreign news content of their major news shows averages from 20 to 25 percent, this total, Arlen feels, is actually reached by two narrow types of reporting: semiofficial accounts of the overseas travels and meetings of our presidents and secretaries of state and largely reflexive, military-oriented coverage of combat situations. "Ongoing interpretive coverage of the world as a whole by U.S. broadcast journalism seems right now to be at a minimum and, despite the profitability of the three networks, shows no signs of becoming more ambitious."[20]

Further, television tends to concentrate for days running on the "big story," such as the hijacking of a TWA plane and taking of U.S. hostages in Beirut, while ignoring significant events else-where. Perhaps this is inevitable in a "headline service," as Walter Cronkite called television news, but it does not help to provide a public, which relies on television as its major source of news, with a fully rounded picture of the world.

One public opinion survey by ABC news found a marked criticism of foreign coverage. Fifty-five percent of those polled agreed with the statement that "television news only does stories about foreign countries when there's a war or some other violent crisis going on."[21] Hodding Carter said the networks "concentrate on showing kids throwing rocks at troops or guns going off or planes bombing or rubble falling. These are the repetitive images that block out the complexities." In addition, he cited the "extraordinary lack of continuity and perspective, which is the shadow of all television news."[22]

There is no doubting, however, the tremendous capacity of television news to focus world attention on some foreign events. Starving Ethiopians had been suffering and enduring hardships for many months, but not until the dramatic color television coverage of their plight appeared on the NBC Evening News night after night were Americans galvanized to support relief efforts. To paraphrase a propaganda maxim, the color television report of an event may be as important as the event itself. The obverse is true as well: an unreported event will have little impact.

Inevitably, much of what happens in the world will go unnoted. Wherever he or she may be, the average person does not have the time or interest to follow all the news from everywhere. As one editor asked, "Who wants to read about Zaire if there is nothing going on there?" Gerald Long of Reuters explained more fully: "The prevalent school of journalism throughout the world is a 'journalism of exception.' In other words, you don't report that everything is fine in Pakistan. You report that there has been an air crash."[23]

Hostility to Western Journalists

The journalism of exception—reporting civil unrest, the coup d'etat, the train wreck, the drought—is at the root of the increasing hostility and antagonism toward Western reporting.

Journalists who work abroad say there is increasing difficulty in gaining access to many parts of the world, particularly Africa, the Middle East, and Asia. Typically, when a political upheaval takes place, one of the first measures authorities take is to close their borders and stop issuing visas to foreigners, including journalists. Even when journalists do obtain visas to some Third World countries, many say they find themselves faced with tight restrictions on their ability to travel, to witness events, and to speak freely with officials and local citizens.

Journalists have had particular difficulty in reporting the war in Chad, the drawn-out conflict between Iran and Iraq, and the troubles between the Sikhs and the Indian government. In the Soviet Union, no Western journalist was able to travel to Gorky when Andrei Sakharov, the physicist and dissident, was reported to be on a hunger strike.[24]

Henry Kamm of the *New York Times* believes that the foreign correspondent is becoming a casualty of the self-assertion of the Third World toward the West. "Demonstrating suspicion toward correspondents and reducing their access to sources of news, much of the Third World is gradually joining the Communist nations in closing itself off from critical inquiry," he wrote.[25]

The field of activity of the Western press is being narrowed increasingly by both formal and informal methods. AP correspondent Mort Rosenblum categorized four forms that such methods can take.

The "Blackout" approach, which seems to be gaining popularity, takes the view that no news at all is better than critical or unflattering reports abroad, so reporters are simply kept out. "Reluctant Coverage" means that reporters are permitted in, but access to news sources or officials is severely limited. The Soviet Union, China, and Eastern European countries are examples. The "Subtle Squeeze" occurs in countries that appear to permit open coverage but actually apply indirect restraints on particular stories. Sometimes correspondents are censored by excessive hospitality that keeps them occupied at some distance from a potentially embarrassing story. The fourth method is "Friendly Persuasion," wherein reporters are not restricted, but efforts are made to influence them in a positive way. American officials have been known to use this method, typified by the press junket—taking reporters to the scene of a news story in hopes they will report favorably on it. Much of what is termed "enlightened public relations" falls within this category.[26]

Reluctant Coverage can often be as effective as the Blackout approach in preventing reportage. On a visit to Tanzania, Henry Kamm was told by a government information official that he should have submitted his precise program in writing long before arrival so that a special government committee could rule on his requests. Because he had not done do, Kamm was told he could see no government official and must not leave the capital at the risk of arrest. The only official help he received for a story on Tanzanian development was a collection of speeches of President Julius Nyerere, the most recent, three years old.[27]

David Lamb of the *Los Angeles Times* agrees that the doors are closing to the Western press. "Across the continent," he wrote of Africa,

> news management is becoming tighter, restrictions on journalists more severe and access to countries more limited. More than a quarter of Black Africa's forty-four governments ban foreign correspondents or admit them infrequently and under such controlled conditions that news, in effect, is managed or blacked out. Others admit journalists only for self-serving group tours, then send them on their way.
>
> Increasingly, Africa views foreign correspondents as a nuisance. They distort the news, governments argue, by dwelling on the negative and the sensational—or, at least, by raising issues that are best ignored in the interests of a developing nation.[28]

After months of protest and violence in South Africa that claimed over 1,000 lives — and all fully reported by Western reporters — the South African government on November 2, 1985, imposed sweeping restraints on foreign press coverage. All reporters, print and broadcast, could cover scenes of unrest only under police supervision. But, most tellingly, pictures and sound recordings of unrest in those areas were banned. If the purpose of the ban was to remove images of violence from foreign television screens, most broadcast journalists said, then it worked. "Nobody wants to be in the position of saying that what the South Africans did has worked," said Peter Jennings of ABC news, "but it has."[29] Subsequently, on June 16, 1986, the tenth anniversary of the uprising in Soweto, the South African government banned the use of comsats for live television coverage of *any* news coming out of South Africa. So while violent confrontation between blacks and whites did not abate in South Africa, the vivid images on television screens did.

A major point of contention is that most developing nations believe the press, including foreign reporters, should serve the host country's national aims, while the Western press believes it must decide for itself what news to report.

Covering wars and civil unrest has always presented special problems, but foreign reporters have faced unusual difficulties in reporting from Beirut and other parts of Lebanon. The very real fears of kidnapping or being killed by various terrorist groups prompted many Western reporters into covering the conflict from Cyprus.

Many reporters are forced to cover individual countries by proxy. Uganda, during its chaotic rule by Idi Amin and Milton Obote, was covered by monitoring Radio Uganda in Nairobi and interviewing diplomats and refugees. Ghana, Guinea, Guinea Bissau, Benin, Equatorial Guinea, and Angola have at various times been covered from afar because they denied access to Western correspondents. When a violent attempted coup took place in Cameroon in 1984, the story was covered by monitoring the Cameroonian radio in Abidjan, Ivory Coast, because no foreign reporters were in the country.

Physical Danger

Foreign correspondents often risk their lives while working in hostile countries. In the Central African Empire in the 1970s, AP reporter Michael Goldsmith was brought handcuffed into the presence of Emperor Jean-Bedel Bokassa I. The ruler suddenly clubbed him to the ground, stepped on his glasses, and began kicking him mercilessly. The rest of the emperor's party joined in, and Goldsmith quickly lost consciousness. He awoke in a tiny detention cell, where he spent the next month. Through diplomatic intercession, Goldsmith was finally released and later said, "What happened to me could happen to any correspondent in countries where the ruler is unstable and regards objective reporting as hostile. I'm concerned that this is something that will spread."[30]

This was indeed a bizarre incident, but many journalists around the world face danger while doing their jobs. During 1985, according to the World Press Freedom Committee, twenty-three journalists were murdered: three died in the Philippines, three in Colombia, the others throughout Latin America, the Middle East, and Africa. In addition, eighty-one other journalists were wounded, 205 jailed, and fifty expelled from countries they were working in.[31]

Louis Boccardi, president of AP, said, "On the international scene, the world continues to grow more difficult to cover. The physical dangers abound. Dozens of journalists have been killed in the last few years . . . and many more injured in the pursuit of a story, their story, wherever it was."[32]

Covering civil wars in the Third World is particularly dangerous for Western correspondents. Lebanon, torn by a protracted civil war, lawlessness, and the Israeli invasion, has been an especially fearful place to work (for any Westerner, not just journalists). A number of journalist-targeted incidents particularly underscore this. Jeremy Levin, Cable News Network Beirut bureau chief, was kidnapped and held by Moslem fundamentalists for over a year until managing to escape. Terry Anderson, Beirut bureau chief of AP, was pulled from his car by gunmen after an early morning tennis match; Islamic Holy War, a Moslem fundamentalist group, took responsibility. Later, an Israeli tank shelled a group of journalists in southern Lebanon, killing a cameraman and a soundman working for CBS News and wounding several other people, reflecting, some said, the animosity between Israel and Beirut-based correspondents. Subsequently, a French TV crew and a French free-lancer were kidnapped. Caught in the violent and emotional crosscurrents between the Israelis, various Lebanese Christian and Moslem groups, and the Syrians and Palestinian factions, the foreign journalists must work with the constant threat of assassination or kidnapping hanging over their heads.

The drawn-out invasion of Uganda by Tanzanian forces was reported mainly from neighboring Kenya because of hostility to foreign journalists from both sides. In the later stages of the conflict that finally drove Idi Amin from power, two West Germans, Hans Bollinger and Wolfgang Stiens, and two Swedes, Arne Lemberg and Earl Bergman, entering Uganda to report on the war were murdered by soldiers loyal to Amin.

Most often, such violence against foreign correspondents is reported sometime after the tragedy. But the murder in Nicaragua of Bill Stewart, a television correspondent for ABC on June 21, 1979, was viewed by millions the same day on the evening television news. While covering the fighting between government troops and Sandinista rebels (both groups had been hostile to American newsmen), Stewart, explaining at a roadblock that he wanted to interview government soldiers, was told to kneel; moments later a soldier walked over and shot him once in the head with a rifle. The whole episode was recorded by an ABC cameraman from a short distance away. This film report, which shocked the nation, also disputed the Nicaraguans' first contention that Stewart was killed while trying to flee.

In El Salvador, names of foreign journalists have appeared on death lists, some have been fired on by government or guerrilla troops, and more than ten have been killed and others wounded. Six U.S. journalists, on their return from a fact-finding trip to Central America, condemned what they described as the suppression of press freedoms and the acts of intimidation and physical violence against domestic and foreign reporters in Guatemala, Nicaragua, and El Salvador.[33]

In Argentina alone during the mid 1970s, more than thirty journalists were killed and 119 others were imprisoned, placed under house arrest, or forced into exile, according to AP and the

Anti-Defamation League. Foreign journalists there were pressured as well. Reporters from ABC, NBC, Voice of America, AP, UPI, and the *Wall Street Journal* were detained and questioned for writing about relatives of missing persons.

Retaliation by the West

Western news organizations and their governments are uncertain how to respond to this treatment of their foreign correspondents. When the Soviet Union expelled AP correspondent George Krimsky from Moscow, the U.S. government retaliated by expelling TASS's correspondent in Washington, D.C. When the Soviets arrested a *Los Angeles Times* reporter and accused him of collecting political and military secrets, both the White House and the U.S. Senate denounced the Soviet Union's action.

The most celebrated case of Soviet harassment of an American journalist occurred on August 23, 1986, when Nicholas Daniloff, Moscow correspondent for *U.S. News and World Report,* was arrested and charged with being a spy one week after Gennadi Zakharov, a Russian associated with the United Nations, was arrested in New York on an espionage charge. A loud and continuous protest over Daniloff being "held as a hostage" came from the U.S. media.

After intensive negotiations, on October 2, 1986, Daniloff was released and flew home, and the following day Zakharov was allowed to leave the United States after pleading "no contest" to the espionage charges. Most journalists regarded Daniloff's release as a straight trade of a journalist for a spy, despite Reagan administration statements that the near simultaneous releases did not constitute a trade. Most journalists said they had hoped to avoid the appearance of an equal exchange, which some said could suggest that Daniloff and other foreign correspondents are spies themselves. Moreover, some felt the Daniloff affair set a precedent so that, in the future, American journalists could be taken hostage and then traded whenever a Soviet spy without diplomatic immunity was apprehended.

Yet the U.S. government does not respond in kind to harass-

ments of American correspondents in the Third World. Stanley
Meisler of the *Los Angeles Times* thinks it should. He wrote:

> What is needed is a recognition of the seriousness of the
> problems, a cry of warning and some tough talk from the
> U.S. government and other governments. The Third World is
> harassing correspondents more and more. In some areas, a
> virtual news blackout exists. This should be unacceptable to
> democratic Western governments that deal with these Third
> World countries. The peoples of these Western societies have
> the right to be informed about the countries with which their
> governments are signing trade, aid, and political agree-
> ments.[34]

On the other hand, some journalists feel strongly that the
Western press's independence from government is compromised
when governments intervene on behalf of foreign correspondents.
William Sheehan of ABC urged caution, saying that the U.S. government should not "directly take up the problems that news gathering organizations have and intercede with other governments. I
feel that the First Amendment precludes such action, that the government's role should neither be in support nor opposition to the
press. . . . It is best that the government not set any agenda to
attempt to find solutions in behalf of the American press."[35]

The difficulties and dangers Western correspondents face from
hostile, authoritarian governments appear to be getting worse, and
a widespread boycott of the Western press in many Third World
countries is seen by some journalists as a distinct possibility. Those
who believe in retaliation point out that Western newspersons
working in authoritarian countries create a unique situation.

Marshall D. Shulman, an expert on the Soviet Union, said:

> The relationship between the government and a newsman
> working out of Moscow and Beijing or any centralized
> authoritarian situation cannot be equated with newsmen
> working in Western capitals. His housing, his ability to travel,
> even his access to food shipments from abroad and his funda-
> mental protection is inextricably related to his government.
> We have to work out new canons to govern the actions of a
> democratic society when it is dealing with an authoritarian
> regime.[36]

Shortcomings of
the Western System

In summary, it may be useful to list some of the major shortcomings and inadequacies of the Western system of foreign news gathering.

Far too few Western journalists and facilities are deployed in the right locations to provide adequate coverage of world news events. Sparsity of local news media in many nations of Africa, Asia, and Latin America compounds the problem because those media are themselves unable to make significant contributions to world news flow.

Serious obstructions to news flow are erected in authoritarian countries by such devices as denial of visas to foreign journalists, censorship, lack of access, and harassment. Ten or fifteen years ago, most reporters covering the Third World would have said that their major problems were logistical — getting to the story and then getting the story out to the world. More recently, better air travel and telex via comsats have improved communications, but the political barriers to news gathering have increased markedly. It is ironic that at a time when travel and communications technology have made even the most distant corners of the world instantly accessible, foreign reporting has become ever more difficult and dangerous.

The limitations and subjectivity of news itself mean that many people somewhere are going to be dissatisfied with how the news is reported. For example, a reporter for the *Los Angeles Times* based in Nairobi, Kenya, is writing for readers some 12,000 miles away in California. His or her stories will be chosen and later edited, not according to what East Africans would prefer to read, but what editors in Los Angeles think their local readers will be interested in knowing. That correspondent in East Africa may regard, say, development problems in Tanzania to be an important story, but the resulting dispatch may be discarded because the editor in Los Angeles thinks there is insufficient interest in the subject.

For news, besides being perishable, is relative and subjective as well as fragmentary and incomplete. Take as an illustration the news of a sudden increase in the price of coffee. In Chicago it means that consumers will be paying 35 cents a pound more for ground coffee — and resenting it very much. To readers in Brazil or the Ivory Coast, the price increase means that coffee-producing nations are receiving a well-deserved break at a time when prices of raw materials from poor nations are lagging further behind those of manufactured goods from rich nations.

Furthermore, it is true, unfortunately, that ethnicity or racism does directly affect news values at times. The deaths of a car full of white South Africans in a road mine explosion will probably attract larger headlines in Western newspapers than the deaths of twenty-five Africans in rioting in black townships.

Also, Western news media, although relatively independent of their own governments, will still tend to report foreign news from the viewpoint of their country's foreign policy concerns. This is not the result of any conspiratorial link between journalists and a state department or a foreign ministry. Rather, the unsurprising fact is that events abroad are of interest to readers in proportion to the ways their own national concerns are involved. Nonetheless, foreign news coverage too often responds to U.S. domestic politics, and this means that often important foreign stories do not get covered because they lack the "local angle" of high reader interest.

From 1948 until 1972, the years when the United States refused to recognize Communist China, U.S. reporting about mainland China was generally sparse and negative. However, after Nixon and Kissinger went to Beijing and the United States played the so-called China card, "Communist China" became the "People's Republic of China" in the U.S. media, and stories about China became friendlier and more positive.

News, it has been said, is what an experienced editor puts in the newspaper. And editors — even those on the same newspaper — do not always agree about the importance, value, or credibility of any particular story.

The Western practice of the journalism of exception, of stressing the disasters, the problems, the upheavals, continues to rankle critics of the press everywhere. In America, many feel the media report far too much negative news. But as Daniel Patrick Moynihan has said, "It is the mark of a democracy that its press is filled with bad news. When one comes to a country where the press is filled with good news, one can be pretty sure that the jails are filled with good men."

But the emphasis on crisis journalism is only one of a long list of complaints and criticism of Western news gathering that has been heard in recent years.

NOTES

1. Sean Kelly, *Access Denied: The Politics of Press Censorship,* Washington Papers, no. 55, 1978, p. 10.
2. Rosemary Righter, *Whose News? Politics, the Press and the Third World* (New York: Times Books, 1978), p. 70.

3. Daniel Drooz, "How to Cover Foreign News," *Editor & Publisher,* Sept. 10, 1983, p. 40.
4. Jim Dunlop, "In America's Interest," *Topic,* June 1983, p. 11.
5. Sally Bedell, "Why TV News Can't Be a Complete View of the World," *New York Times,* Aug. 8, 1982, Entertainment section, p. 1.
6. Ralph Kliesch, "A Vanishing Species: The American Newsman Abroad," *Overseas Press Club Directory* (New York, 1975), p. 17.
7. "Chad Gets Largest Group of Journalists Ever," *AP Log,* Sept. 5, 1983, p. 4.
8. Shailendra Ghorpade, "Foreign Correspondents Cover Washington for the World," *Journalism Quarterly* 61, no. 3 (Autumn 1984):667.
9. George Gerbner and George Marvanyi, "The Many Worlds of the World's Press," *Journal of Communication* 27 (Winter 1977):52–66.
10. Mort Rosenblum, *Coups and Earthquakes: Reporting the World for America* (New York: Harper and Row, 1979), p. 8.
11. "International Problems Top U.S. Concerns in Poll," *New York Times,* Feb. 16, 1986, p. 3.
12. Sally Bedell Smith, "New TV Technologies Are Starting to Change the Nation's Viewing Habits," *New York Times,* Oct. 9, 1985, p. 10.
13. Ibid.
14. Drooz, "How to Cover Foreign News."
15. Lester Markel and Audrey March, *Global Challenge to the United States* (Cranbury, N.Y.: Associated University Presses, 1976), pp. 121–23.
16. Ibid.
17. Xan Smiley, "Misunderstanding Africa," *Atlantic,* September 1982, p. 70.
18. Ibid.
19. Michael J. Arlen, "The Air: The Eyes and Ears of the World," *The New Yorker,* Jan. 6, 1975, pp. 52ff.
20. Ibid.
21. Bedell, "Why TV News."
22. Ibid.
23. Righter, *Whose News?,* p. 70.
24. Richard Bernstein, "Western Reporters Face Steadily Rising Barriers," *International Herald Tribune,* July 28, 1984, p. 1.
25. Henry Kamm, "Third World Rapidly Turning into a Closed World for the Foreign Correspondent," *New York Times,* Jan. 14, 1976, p. 3.
26. Rosenblum, *Coups and Earthquakes,* pp. 98ff.
27. Kamm, "Third World."
28. See David Lamb, *The Africans* (New York: Random House, 1982), pp. 243–77.
29. Peter J. Boyer, "South Africa and TV: The Coverage Changes," *New York Times,* Dec. 29, 1985, p. 1.
30. "Beating the Press," *Newsweek,* Aug. 29, 1977, p. 54.
31. Caroline Moorehead, "Rights Groups Seek to Cut Killings of Journalists," *Times* of London, Dec. 2, 1985, p. 3.
32. Mark Fitzgerald, "A Dangerous Affair," *Editor & Publisher,* Nov. 2, 1985, p. 18.
33. William A. Blair, "Latin Press Policy Assailed by Group," *New York Times,* April 2, 1982, p. 6.
34. Stanley Meisler, "Covering the Third World (or trying to)," *Columbia Journalism Review,* November/December 1978, p. 38.
35. I. William Hill, "News Execs Testify on Information Policy," *Editor & Publisher,* June 25, 1977, p. 12.
36. Deirdre Carmody, "Press and Its Independence," *New York Times,* Feb. 8, 1979, p. 2.

8

Controversy over a "New World Information Order"

> The present information order, based as it is on a quasi-monopolistic concentration of the power to communicate in the hands of a few developed nations, is incapable of meeting the aspirations of the international community.
>
> —*Mustapha Masmoudi*

> New World Information Order: "the constant reiteration of the forever unclear."
>
> —*William Harley*

IN Freetown, Sierra Leone, a group of women and children stand immobilized in front of a large television monitor outside the state-owned broadcasting studios. Several of the women, wearing traditional *temle* and *lapa* of colorfully patterned cloth, are carrying babies in slings on their backs. All are transfixed by an episode of "The Flintstones."

An item in the *Times of India* about a Cambodian refugee camp in Thailand carries a Reuters credit line.

Three young men in Riyadh, Saudi Arabia, cluster around a television set and watch Sylvester Stallone as "Rambo" on a video cassette smuggled into the country from London.

In Latin America, serious scholars write academic studies about sinister capitalistic values with such titles as "How to Read Donald Duck: Mass Communication and Colonialism."

These media snapshops from around the Third World are more than merely vivid vignettes that catch the attention of a Western traveler. They are in fact illustrations of the issues at the heart of the extraordinary controversy over the control of the flow of global news and mass culture, a controversy that has aroused the heated concern of journalists, diplomats, and academics in many nations.

This "great debate," which usually pits Western newsmen against Third World and Communist political leaders, involves scathing attacks on the West's traditional methods of collecting and distributing international news and has led to repeated calls for a "New World Information Order" (NWIO)—a vague but radical reordering of the international communication system.

The disagreements and disputes, which started in the early 1970s and have slowly but not completely abated, reflect the widening communication disparities between the West and the poor nations of the Third World that consider themselves recipients of a one-way flow of communication. The controversy is in large part political and ideological and stems from power and economic relationships.

On the one hand, the "information societies" of the West have been expanding their ability to communicate globally. By comparison, underdeveloped nations have inadequate media systems and are largely passive recipients of the increasing flow of global communication. In addition to news, this includes a deluge of mass culture products—motion pictures, television programs, video and audio cassettes, records, and various publications—much of it coming from the United States and Britain. Communist bloc nations as well as other nations are sensitive to this influx also. Some Canadians, for example, feel overwhelmed by the media outpourings from their giant neighbor to the south.

This widening breach results from differences in political and economic structures as well as conflicting concepts of media controls. The Western model of journalism is sharply criticized and largely rejected by Communist nations and the new autocracies of the Third World. As a British journalist put it:

> The freedom of the Anglo-Amercian press to roam the world, criticizing, commenting, and generally poking its nose into the affairs of most non-Western societies, is something we

have taken for granted since the end of the Second World War. The obeisance to democratic ideas at the time elevated the rights of the foreign press into one of the lesser principles of international life, like diplomatic immunity or airline agreements. It was a principle subscribed to by all non-Communist countries, even where the freedom of their domestic press came to be curtailed. But now we are fast approaching a point where not only is it honored more in the breach than in the observance, but the principle itself is under direct attack.[1]

The Western approach to news gathering was embodied in Article 19 of the United Nations' "Universal Declaration of Human Rights," voted in 1948, that stated in part, "Everyone has the right to freedom of opinion and expression—and to seek, receive, and impart information and ideas through any medium and regardless of frontiers." Western journalists have long insisted that there must be a free flow of communication to accomplish this. Peoples everywhere, they said, should have access to information, especially information that affects their security, their well-being, their destinies; therefore, journalists must have an unimpeded right to collect and distribute news anywhere in the world.

This view, for a considerable time, was the official position of the United Nations, and especially the United Nations Educational, Scientific and Cultural Organization (UNESCO), which has a special concern with international communication. But by 1972, the concept of free flow of information was under attack, as typified by declarations both by the UNESCO General Conference and the UN General Assembly concerning direct-broadcast satellites, whereby television programming is sent by communications satellites directly to an individual television receiver, bypassing ground receiving stations. The UNESCO group, by a vote or 55 to 7, with the United States voting against and twenty-two nations abstaining, adopted a draft resolution on satellite broadcasting that subscribed to the necessity of *prior agreements* between nations before direct satellite broadcasting occurs. This was the first significant retreat from unqualified support for global free flow.

Within weeks, a UN General Assembly vote directed the UN Outer Space Committee to formulate guiding principles for direct-broadcast satellites. Impetus for the action was the Soviet Union's proposal that any international agreement on satellites stipulate regulations against broadcasting into sovereign nations without permission. The UN General Assembly vote for adoption was 101 to 1, the United States alone dissenting. (These votes restricting free flow of television signals came against a backdrop of international shortwave radio, which of course has long sent a cacophony of communication across national frontiers. See Chap. 6.)

These actions set the pattern for what was to come. These international bodies, with a majority from Third World nations, have been modifying the principle of free flow by espousing the view that international communicators must obtain *prior consent* of the nation into which their journalists and news reports may move. In the Western view, this is but a short step to the authoritarian principle that each government has the inherent right to control news entering and leaving its borders.

UNESCO has been a leading forum, but not the only one, for this ongoing controversy, which has involved, in addition to UNESCO representatives, communication scholars and their associations and journals and professional journalists and their organizations, such as the International Press Institute, Inter American Press Association, International Organization of Journalists, World Press Freedom Committee. Much has been written and many speeches have been delivered as the controversy has swelled at times with increasing passion and acrimony. A large part of the rhetoric has been just that—rhetoric—but the amount of serious research into the issues raised has been surprisingly small until recently. The late Ithiel de Sola Pool, exasperated over the controversy, wrote, "One could fill a volume with heated quotations from unhappy nationalists, guilt-ridden Westerners, worried reactionaries, and angry radicals attacking the free flow of information as a Western plot to impose its culture on helpless people."[2]

Be that as it may, the controversy has continued despite efforts to accommodate and resolve the differences.

Arguments for a New World Information Order

The term "New World Information Order" includes both a wide ranging critique of the Western news system as well as a rather vague "program" with few specifics and no timetable for rectifying the situation. One critic called it a "slogan in search of a program."

NWIO advocates point out that a few Western nations provide

most of the world's news coverage, entertainment, and advertising. Much of the news coverage, they say, is controlled by a few multinational news agencies. This is unacceptable because the agencies (Associated Press, United Press International, Reuters, Agence France Presse) devote too little attention to the domestic affairs of developing nations and foster a negative image of those countries. This they do, the argument runs, by focusing on sensational and disastrous events while ignoring positive events, particularly development issues. In addition, NWIO advocates charge that commercial advertising and mass culture products foster biases in favor of the industrialized world and multinational corporations, thereby threatening their cultural identity.

For some of the more radical critics, the remedy is to restrict the free international flow of information, particularly by curbing the activities of Western news agencies. Specifically, proposals have been made to license journalists, impose international codes of journalistic ethics, inhibit advertising, and extend government control over the press. In this way, they hope to limit outside influences and keep a tighter control over news and information flowing in and out of their countries. (The Soviet Union has consistently supported various proposals for restricting press freedoms.)

Not all developing nations see a NWIO in such negative terms. Many believe that the gaps in news and communication capacity are real and should be addressed by practical development efforts, including more aid from the West. These countries seek cooperation, not confrontation, with the developed nations.

After the early concern with direct-broadcast satellites, the controversy zeroed in on international news flow and the Western media themselves. The Third World has not lacked spokesmen, and one of the most widely quoted has been Mustapha Masmoudi of Tunisia.[3]

Information in the world, Masmoudi said, is characterized by basic imbalances, reflecting the general economic and social inequities that affect the international community. First, there is a flagrant quantitative imbalance between North and South, created by the disparity between the volume of news and information emanating from the developed world and intended for the developing countries and the volume of the flow in the opposite direction. Masmoudi charged that 80 percent of the world news flow comes from the four major Western nations (AP, UPI, Reuters, AFP), but that these agencies devote too little attention to the Third World. So, without news agencies of their own, the Third World is dependent on the "big four" for news about themselves and their neighbors.

But the Western media, he said, are oblivious to the real concerns of the Third World nations, which are relegated to the status of mere consumers of news and information, which are sold to them like any other commodity. Masmoudi said the Western media tend to stress the most unfavorable news about poor nations — crises, coups, civil wars, terrorism, street demonstrations — "even holding them up to ridicule."

The present-day information system, Masmoudi said, "enshrines a form of political, economic, and cultural colonialism which is reflected in the often tendentious interpretation of news concerning the developing countries. The Western media are selective in what they report and the criteria used are based on the political and economic interests of the transnational systems and the countries where those multinational corporations are located."

The arguments of Masmoudi, and others, can be summarized thus:

• The world news agencies "monopolize" the news.

• Alien and irrelevant values and life-styles of the West are imposed on developing societies through a "one-way flow" that amounts to "cultural imperialism," thus threatening traditional cultures.

• News from the Third World is often negative and distorted.

• Existing lines of communication are vertical, running from North to South, and there is little news exchange, say, from Asia to Africa, or vice versa.

• Developing nations cannot afford a free press, and freedom from want must come before freedom of expression. Hence, the media must be recruited to serve the broad national interests of development.

• Developing nations must control not only their own media but also the flow of news and information in and out of their own countries.

To overcome this perceived domination by Western media, NWIO advocates argue that Third World must establish its "right to communicate" — to talk back. This means "disestablishing"

Western communication rights, which are based on "individualistic considerations to the detriment of collective needs." Freedom to communicate, they say, should no longer be limited to those who own or control the media.

To achieve their desired changes, a series of "musts" were laid down:

• The Third World *must not* be shown in an unfavorable light.

• The world media *must* reserve more time and space for news of developing nations.

• News flow to a country *must not* clash with that country's cultural and moral values.

• The content, volume, and intensity of flow between developed and developing countries *must* be "free and equitable."

All of this can be achieved, it is argued, by a New World Information Order that calls for (1) regulation of the right to information by preventing abusive use of the right to access of information, (2) definition of appropriate criteria to govern truly objective news selection, (3) regulation of the collection, processing, and transmission of information across national frontiers, (4) enforcement through domestic legislation and a new supranational agency of a proposed international journalistic code and penalties, including the licensing of journalists, and (5) assurance that a state can have published a communique rectifying and supplementing the false or incomplete information already disseminated. Although there have been numerous variations on these themes, this is in essence the argument for a New World Information Order.

Underlying all of this are the frustrations and impotence of the Third World in the face of economic and power imbalances in the world. By 1970, at the end of the heralded UN Development Decade, the poverty gap between rich and poor nations had widened and dependence on the West for technology, development aid, financing, and trade had increased and is still increasing today, especially in light of heavy debt burdens of many Third World nations. Then, in 1974, came a call for a New International Economic Order, which was in essence a demand for a fairer share of the world's resources. If the developed nations were indeed exploiting the decolonized Third World, as charged, it followed that the Western media must somehow be playing a role in that exploitation.

The new nations had turned their attention to communication

media at the Fourth Non-Aligned Summit in Algiers in 1973 in the context of a program for economic cooperation. Their own media, they agreed, must be strengthened as part of the efforts to "eliminate the harmful consequences of the colonial era." So, from the outset, the attack on Western media has been explicitly associated with the call for a new economic order. Not unexpectedly, soon afterward came the call for a New World Information Order to restructure a global media system whose reporting was widely believed to be responsible, at least in part, for the West's failure to respond to the trade, aid, and financial needs of developing nations, many of which had retrogressed economically and politically since decolonization.

Failures to develop were blamed on "economic dependence." This widely accepted conventional wisdom of Third World apologists was reflected in the influential MacBride report:

> Confronted by the sheer might of the richer nations, the developing countries found that they were partners, perhaps, but in a very unequal relationship. The better equipped still carried disproportionate weight in political, economic and scientific affairs, as well as a preponderant impact on communication. Flooded by a one way flow of information and entertainment produced in the industrialized countries, the developing countries came to realize the dangers of cultural dependence. They grew dissatisfied with the way in which the communication systems worked and wanted greater access to the media. This generated frustration and a mood of rejection that has taken the form of active discontent with information systems and protests against external domination.[4]

Disparities in communication capability, then, were blamed for the Third World's plight (not the disastrous economic policies, political corruption, and misguided rule of the nations involved that many leaders now admit to).

Among some of the NWIO advocates, a conspiracy was clearly evident: the Western media were accused of being malevolently and cynically manipulated by their own governments to deliberately keep poor developing nations in a perpetual state of dependence and economic servitude. Other proponents of the new "order" want to restructure the world's media system to help achieve a more just and equitable economic system and thus to aid and help achieve social justice. But to the West, where the media are largely privately owned (and in the case of broadcasting, often publicly owned), the press exists to inform the people and to protect liberty against the abuses of governments. Liberty is not the same as social justice, and Western journalists say that when press freedom is sacrificed for some vague social goal, then political liberty and human rights disappear.

Arguments Opposing
a New Information Order

Journalists and political leaders in Western democracies have reacted in various ways to this verbal assault on Western mass media. Some reject it out of hand as a cynical effort to politicize international news and to justify and gain international respectability for government control of news and censorship. Others concede a few of the charges and reject others, but very few journalists in the West and not many independent journalists in the Third World, either, have bought the whole argument for a revamped news system.

Many thoughtful journalists and others concede that there are real bases for Third World complaints but are opposed to the proposals to implement the "order." It was agreed that real disparities in news flow exist, the non-Western nations do receive a lot more news and information than they send out, and that much of their entertainment and mass culture comes from the West. And certainly the poorer nations are being bypassed by new technology in telecommunications. Many in the West agree that news media should report more Third World news and do it with more understanding and regard for the views of other nations.

Yet, the coups, the economic disasters, the corruption, and the civil wars must also be reported, regardless of where they occur. Agreed, the Western press should provide more comprehensive, sustained reporting of foreign regions and with more historical perspective. This is necessary because the Third World must often rely on Western media to find out what is happening in their own and neighboring countries. But further, people in the West would benefit from a better balanced flow of news.

Rosemary Righter agreed that critics of the existing system have a point when they say their affairs are badly reported and that

Western media either ignore them or ignore the news they consider important, stressing instead the "bad news." But the Western agencies, she says, "cannot and do not force their wares on unwilling buyers."[5] In many Third World nations, individual newspapers and broadcasters are not permitted to subscribe directly to Western news agencies; rather, government news agencies are the clients and they redistribute the agency news to local media, thus acting as a real or potential censor. Government too is the principal purchaser of incoming movies and television programs. Thus, Western news and entertainment are not imposed on unwilling nations but are usually sought out and paid for by official agencies. So the picture of the millions in poor nations being inundated by unwanted alien information is fanciful. The governments are very much in control.

Righter adds, "It is not only the dominance of the Western press that is under attack; the model of a free press is being rejected as alien and undesirable. This goes beyond the familiar arguments of national leaders that their societies are too vulnerable to permit an independent press to function freely. It has led to pressure for control over the activities of the international press."[6]

Western critics, then, see the New World Information Order as not just a critique of certain news practices but as essentially an attack on free and independent journalism. An independent press, they argue, makes self-government and democracy possible, and a central problem of journalism around the world is to establish and maintain independent news media that are able to report and criticize their own governments without retaliation or suppression of their freedoms. Few countries have such media, so the free, Western international media play a surrogate role of providing reliable information to peoples living in nations without independent newspapers.

Further, as groups like Amnesty International attest, a free press plays a particularly useful role in publicizing the plight of political prisoners worldwide and of reporting violations of human rights. Yet the whole thrust of the NWIO is to provide legitimacy for government control of information.

As Charles Krauthammer wrote:

> One of the two purposes of the NWIO is to improve communications within the Third World. That we can support. The other is to provide international sanction for official control of domestic and foreign news sources. Such control al-

ready exists in the Soviet system and in many parts of the
Third World. UNESCO declarations will not make it any
easier for journalists to get into Outer Mongolia or Argentin-
ian prisons. Nor will it make it appreciably harder, but it will
grant the international legitimacy that censors always crave
and might encourage those nations currently wavering to
choose press restrictions.[7]

Declarations and policy statements made in the United Nations and UNESCO or other bodies are, of course, nonbinding on
members, but some nations otherwise hesitant to take a certain
action may find courage in numbers or feel morally justified if a
declaration or code adopted by a hundred other nations existed.
The end effect, some feel, would be to justify and protect repres-
sive actions by authoritarian regimes. That is why many have opposed the NWIO.

Some of the NWIO charges against the Western news media
are fallacious and do not stand up under close examination. The
big four Western news agencies do not carry anywhere near the 80
percent of the world's news, as is frequently charged, and they do
not neglect the Third World. For example, a monitoring of AP,
UPI, Reuters, and AFP news services in Asia found that these
agencies carry a daily average of 100,000 words of Third World
news — five times what nineteen representative Asian newspapers in
the region actually printed. Further, Asian newspapers were found
to carry very little news about Africa, even though it was available,
and vice versa. The same is true about Latin America in regard to
regional news from Asia and Africa.[8]

Numerous advocates of the NWIO come from nations that do
not support press freedom within their own countries. Indonesian
journalist Moctor Lubis, twice jailed by his own government, said,
"I have much less patience and less respect for the spokesmen from
the Third World who demand at the international level a 'free and
balanced' flow of information and news but who are completely
silent about the non-existence of a free and balanced flow of news
and information within their own countries, between the power
elite which rules and the masses of the population." It should be
stressed that within developing countries that are calling for a new
information order are many journalists, editors, and broadcasters
who support the concepts of information freedom as set out by the
UN Declaration of Rights of 1948.

The Belgrade meeting of UNESCO in October 1978 was expected to provide a compromise between those who view news communication as an aspect of political liberty and those who view it as an adjunct of political power. Instead, it became apparent that NWIO advocates wanted an international charter with rules to govern news flow. Such a charter would apparently place restrictions on the free flow of news, especially from the major Western news agencies, and provide for licensing of journalists, an international code of ethics, restrictions on advertising, and other press controls.

A move toward reconciliation of differences was made by UNESCO's International Commission for the Study of Communication Problems. Chaired by Sean MacBride, the sixteen-member group met for two years, issuing its final report in February 1980.[9] The report recommended that journalists have free access to all news sources, both official and unofficial, and that all censorship be abolished. While supporting journalists' rights of access to news, the report accepted Third World concerns about their "colonial domination" of news distribution. Private ownership of media came in for some harsh words: "Special attention should be devoted to obstacles and restrictions which derive from the concentration of ownership, public and private, from commercial influences on the press and broadcasting or from private and governmental advertising. The problem of financial condition under which the media operate should be critically reviewed, and measures elaborated to strengthen editorial independence."[10] The MacBride commission did not resolve the issues, of course, and was in fact criticized by both sides.

Concerned at this turn of events, some sixty leaders of print and broadcasting media from twenty countries met at Talloires, France, in May 1981 and pledged to fight efforts of UNESCO to set up the information order. The "Declaration of Talloires" called press freedom a "basic right," and participants said they were resolved to resist any encroachment on it. UNESCO was urged to "abandon attempts to regulate news content and formulate rules for press conduct," insisting this violated its own charter, the Universal Declaration of Human Rights, and the Helsinki Declaration on Human Rights and was inconsistent with the UN charter.

The declaration attacked the NWIO as politically motivated and specifically opposed plans to license journalists through the device of identity cards and opposed calls for an international code of ethics, saying such codes could only be drawn up by the press itself and must be voluntary. The "abolition of all censorship and other forms of arbitrary control of information and opinion," was called for on the basis that "peoples' rights to news and information must not be abridged," and the demand was made that journalists have the right of access to all sources of news and information, including people who disagree with a government's policy.[11]

The Talloires meeting was important because it was the first time Western and other free media representatives had taken a united stand against efforts by Soviet bloc and Third World countries to regulate global news.

The Western critique was reinforced by some research studies. Robert Stevenson, one of the participants in an international analysis of news coverage by press, radio and television in twenty-nine countries commented on the "World of the News" study:

> Let us begin by noting what this study does *not* show. It does not show that Western media and news agencies ignore the Third World. It does not show that they single out the Third World for unfair negative coverage. It does not show that they see the Third World through a filter of cultural bias. It does not show that Third World media are hostage to a Western news monopoly. . . . Assertions that the Western media and news agencies ignore the Third World are not true. About one-third of foreign news in Northern media systems originates in the Third World; in Third World countries, two-thirds to three-quarters of all foreign news is from other Third World countries.
>
> This study suggests that the ideological rhetoric is misplaced in three ways. First, many of the charges against the Western media and news services are without evidence to support them. Second, the lack of difference among media of very different political systems argues against the theory of cultural imperialism. And, third, much of the rhetoric addresses outdated questions. . . . This study helps clear the air of the pseudo debate.[12]

On the other hand, another recent study by Professor C. Anthony Giffard suggests that qualitative difference exists in coverage of the more developed and less developed countries. The composite picture of Third World countries is that of being more prone to internal conflicts and crises, armed conflicts, disasters, etc. (Journalists would argue that this is the kind of news these nations have been making.) But Giffard adds, "This does not mean that developed nations are immune to these afflictions. For the most part, the same categories of news dominate the coverage of the industrialized world. The difference is that other kinds of news help leaven the mix."[13]

Efforts at Conciliation and Compromise

During the 1980s, the controversy continued but in a more moderate and reasonable tone. Among Western critics of the NWIO was a growing consensus that the basic problems were those of both improving the media systems of Third World nations and providing more diversity and variety of news outlets for the global dissemination of news and entertainment.

Both sides seemed more willing to find ways to conciliate their differences. UNESCO policymakers said the organization was shifting its activities toward concrete projects that would improve communication media and technical training for journalists in developing nations. The vehicle was the new International Program for Development of Communications (IPDC), the brainchild of William Harley, a U.S. State Department consultant. The industrialized nations were to provide concrete financial assistance for projects that would improve the Third World's ability to communicate. At an IPDC meeting in Acapulco, Mexico, in 1982, some fifteen such proposals were considered, including $1.5 million for developing national and regional news agencies in Africa, $1.2 million to create a regional center for communication training and development in Africa, $220,000 to plan satellite systems for news and program exchanges among Arab states, $250,000 for an Arab states center for broadcasting training, and $350,000 to develop a news exchange program for Asia and the Pacific.[14] In May 1984, the organization allocated $1.8 million for forty-two projects, which were priced at $42 million. Most were given token sums of less than $50,000.

Future success of IPDC was dependent on continued Western financial support. This was not at all assured, in part because of American and British withdrawal from UNESCO. Some Western journalists criticized the fact that all of the initial IPDC projects appeared to strengthen government media and did little for independent media. Cushrow Irani, publisher of the Indian daily, *The Statesman,* and chairman of the International Press Institute, charged that the United States was supporting projects contrary to the aims of a free press. He called U.S. support of the IPDC "naive" and mistakenly based on a "fear of interfering in the internal affairs of other countries."[15]

For their part, U.S. news agencies and other media have shown a clear willingness to report more Third World news and to do so with more sensitivity. Moreover, Western journalists joined efforts to help train Third World journalists. At a second Talloires conference of ninety representatives of media from twenty-five countries held in September 1983, a "List of Talloires" was released, enumerating more than 300 programs in over seventy countries that included training, educational, exchange, intern, and fellowship programs for journalists in various countries. In 1984, for example, the American Society of Newspaper Editors launched a series of internship programs for Third World journalists. Other similar efforts were started.

Probably a more significant development has been the expansion of alternative and regional news agencies that can supplement and add variety to news coming from Western news organizations. The oldest alternative agency is the Non-Aligned News Agencies Pool (NANAP), which dates from the Fourth Non-Aligned Summit in Algiers in 1973. Although about eighty nations were involved, Yugoslavia and its agency, Tanjug, has been the moving force of the pool.

A more recent and important example is the Inter Press Service Third World News Agency (IPS).[16] IPS is a nonprofit cooperative based in Rome specializing in Third World news, which it distributes to media in Europe and North America. With bureaus or correspondents in sixty countries, two-thirds of them in the Third World, IPS maintains exchanges with thirty national news agencies. The focus is on news relating to Third World development instead of spot news. Other alternative agencies that have been adding diversity to global news flow include Pacific News Service, Gemini News Service, and South-North News Service.[17]

After twenty years of planning and consultations among African nations after the birth of the Organization of African Unity in 1963, the Pan African News Agency (PANA) was finally inaugurated in May 1983, with the major objective "to promote an effective exchange of political, economic, social, and cultural information among member states" and to "liberate African information from imperialist domination, foreign monopolies and resolutely gear it towards the promotion of development."[18] PANA can provide an important service for African journalism if it can overcome the built-in problems of lack of professionalism, shortage of funds and telecommunications, low credibility due to the heavy involvement of government news agencies, and political differences between African nations.

Another indication of the conciliatory direction of the discussion is that the cries of "cultural imperialism" (i.e., the flooding of American mass culture around the world) have receded as more and more nations have begun producing and exporting their own mass culture products. Nations such as Mexico, Egypt, and India, for example, have been major exporters of entertainment programming for their regions. Britain limits American shows, excluding movies, to 14 percent of all television programs. France announced the formation of its second commercial network, which would be required to run at least 450 hours of French shows and video in its first year. The world has available an increasing variety of programming sold more and more across international markets.[19]

The diplomatic event that markedly quieted the controversy over a NWIO was the decision of the U.S. government to withdraw from UNESCO on January 1, 1985. Britain, another of the key founders of the controversial organization forty years earlier, followed at the end of 1985. Singapore also withdrew. Principal reasons given were that the 160-nation organization had become politicized, focusing on ideological concerns rather than on global problems of literacy, education, science, and media development. The Reagan administration argued it would not support an organization espousing positions that ran counter to our basic principles and values. UNESCO was also accused of being a bloated, inefficient bureaucracy, as 80 percent of its budget of $347 million was spent on its Paris headquarters rather than in the developing nations. Most U.S. media supported the action, agreeing with an editorial in the *New York Times:*

> Every meeting became an anti-Western rally. Worse, some "cultural" programs were turned to antidemocratic purposes. The Third World's justifiable interest in communications technology, for example, was transformed into a "new world information order," an effort to legitimize state manipulation of international news. Though the effort was blunted, it was destructive and demeaning for democrats to have to defend their free institutions and to have to pretend that the Soviet Union and most other advocates of a new order were legitimate partners in the protection of press freedoms.[20]

A number of U.S. journalists and diplomats who had worked closely with UNESCO strongly disagreed with the withdrawal, arguing that Western influence in the international communication issues would be seriously diminished. Ironically, the U.S. withdrawal came at a time when Western influence on the NWIO controversy was reasserting itself. The U.S. government maintains an observer status in UNESCO and could return in the future.

By the mid-1980s, the long-running debate was clearly winding down, even though the conditions that precipitated the controversy still remained. But the world had changed and so had international communication.

NOTES

1. Martin Woollacott, "Western News-gathering: Why the Third World Has Reacted," *Journalism Studies Review* 1, no. 1 (June 1976):12.
2. Ithiel de Sola Pool, "Direct Broadcast Satellites and the Integrity of National Cultures," *Control of the Direct Broadcast Satellite: Values in Conflict* (Palo Alto, Calif.: Aspen Institute, 1974), pp. 27–35.
3. Masmoudi's remarks are taken from a 1978 UNESCO paper he prepared for UNESCO's International Commission for the Study of Communication Problems and chaired by Sean MacBride.
4. *Many Voices, One World* (MacBride Report), abridged edition (New York: UNESCO, 1984), p. 55.
5. Rosemary Righter, "The Roots of the Controversy," *World Press Review,* October 1981, p. 42.
6. Ibid.
7. Charles Krauthammer, "Brave News World," *New Republic,* May 14, 1981, p. 23.
8. Wilbur Schramm and Erwin Atwood, *Circulation of News in the Third World: A Study of Asia* (Hong Kong: Chinese University Press, 1981).

9. *Many Voices, One World* (Paris: UNESCO, 1980).

10. Ibid., p. 217.

11. Paul Lewis, "West's News Organizations Vow to Fight Unesco on Press Curbs," *New York Times,* May 15, 1981, p. 1.

12. Robert L. Stevenson, "Pseudo Debate," *Journal of Communication* (Winter 1984):134, 137.

13. C. Anthony Giffard, "Developed and Developing Nation News in U.S. Wire Service Files to Asia," *Journalism Quarterly* 61, no. 1 (Spring 1984):19.

14. "IPDC Development Proposals Emphasize Government Efforts," *Presstime,* November 1981, p. 17.

15. Barbara Crossette, "U.S. Accused of Favoring Curbs on Free Press," *New York Times,* Nov. 21, 1981.

16. C. Anthony Giffard, "The Inter Press Service: New Information for a New Order," *Journalism Quarterly* 62, no. 1 (Spring 1985):17.

17. Elise Burroughs, "Fledgling News Services Cover the Third World," *Presstime,* August 1983, pp. 14–16.

18. Paul A. V. Ansah, "The Pan-African News Agency—A Preliminary Profile" (paper prepared for the 14th IAMCR Conference in Prague, August 1984), p. 1.

19. Philip S. Gutis, "American TV Isn't Traveling So Well," *New York Times,* Feb. 2, 1986, section E, p. 5.

20. "Little Education, Science or Culture," *New York Times,* Dec. 16, 1983, p. 26.

9

Moving Together or Further Apart?

The world is moving in two directions: one is toward the narrowing of distances through travel, increasing interchange between scientists (who take a world view of problems such as the exploration of space, ecology, population); the other is toward the shutting down of frontiers, the ever more jealous surveillance by governments and police of individual freedom.

—Stephen Spender

IN 1957, an accident at a Soviet nuclear waste dump in the Ural mountains contaminated 25,000 square miles of land, yet it took months for just the news of that event to spread outside the country.

Almost thirty years later, in April 1986, another Soviet nuclear accident occurred—at the Chernobyl plant near Kiev. Within two days, Swedish monitoring stations were reporting high levels of radiation, and word of the accident quickly spread around the world despite Soviet efforts to keep a lid on the events.

Communication technology made the difference in the diffusion of the news of the two events, mainly the presence of both military and civilian satellites capable of photographing the stricken reactor plant from space. The dramatic pictures were flashed by news agencies around the world, again by satellites, reaching even into Communist countries that were not telling their own citizens what had happened. Marshall McLuhan's electronic global village, predicted in 1964, had indeed arrived.

This was another example of how satellite technology has changed the scope of international communication. It has made it increasingly difficult for authoritarian governments to keep important news from their citizens—and from the world.

For expanded international communication is at the heart of a major historic trend of the last half of the twentieth century: the modernization of the world through global dissemination of technical, scientific, economic, and social information and practices emanating from Western society. Even though nation states, and particularly the two superpowers, still make the crucial decisions, we are becoming a rudimentary world community. More and more, it is apparent that cooperation is more important than confrontation in dealing with global concerns.

Two developments in communications are crucial in the process: the arrival of long-distance, high-speed transmission of information (including color television, as typified by the communication satellite) and personalized communications gadgets (such as the personal computer and video cassette recorder), enabling individuals to seek out information and to select their own entertainment. Both represent considerable challenges to authoritarian governments that seek to control and censor information and cultural fare.

The expanded capacity to communicate information rapidly around a world that has become ever-more interdependent, as the Chernobyl accident showed, has begun to erase some differences and improve understanding among diverse societies.

The better educated and more affluent people of most nations—the media users—know more about the outside world and have access to more information than ever before. The educated elites of the developing nations, small though they are in number, travel more and are more conversant with world affairs than their predecessors under colonialism.

The international news system, despite its inadequacies, moves a great deal of information, data, and pictures at much faster speeds than ever before. A major world news event, enhanced by color television pictures via comsats, frequently has immense and dramatic impact. But words and pictures do not always bring understanding; in fact, just the opposite often results in this diverse and heterogeneous world.

The West's version of world news, largely gathered and disseminated by American and West European journalists, often antagonizes and annoys non-Western governments and peoples, despite their clear dependence on these sources of information.

As the previous chapter indicates, many question the validity of the current system of international news communication and would replace it with a "new order" that would significantly alter the ways that news is exchanged. The poorer nations' frustrations and antagonisms toward Western media cannot be separated from the economic disparities between rich and poor countries, many of them former colonies.

To deal with their formidable problems of poverty, massive debt, economic stagnation, illiteracy, and sometimes famine and disease, some leaders would harness communication to assist governments in dealing with these pressing issues—a clear invocation of the Developmental concept of the press (see Chap. 2). But under the Western concept, the press must be free of government to maintain liberty, to make democracy possible. Liberty is not the same as social justice or economic equality, and history shows that when press freedom is sacrificed for some "greater good," then political liberty and human rights usually disappear.

To the Western journalist, the press must be independent of authority, not an instrument of government, so that it can report the news and expose the abuses of governments at home and abroad. Now more than ever, governments need watching. For whether democratic or authoritarian, only governments—not multinational corporations or media conglomerates—have the power to start wars, nuclear or conventional, to conscript soldiers and send them off to dubious foreign adventures, to punish dissidents, to establish gulags.

Modern history is strewn with regimes marred by incompetence, venality, corruption, and brutality. Masmoudi's charges notwithstanding, some journalists believe the world's free press has done far too little, rather than too much, critical reporting about economic failures and political abuses, especially in the Third World. This basic impasse over the proper purpose of international news communication and the relations between the press and government will undoubtedly continue.

Besides these philosophical differences, the onrush of rapid technological change is further widening the gap between the rich and poor nations. Lacking skilled workers and an industrial base, including investment capital, and without a literate and educated middle class, the poor nations are unable to participate fully in the information revolution. When most of a country's population still live as illiterate peasants on subsistence agriculture, as is true in much of Africa, Asia, and parts of Latin America, terms like "transnational data flows," "free flow of information," or even a "new world information order" have little practical meaning. For the communication revolution is coming about through education, communication, and dynamic free market economies, all in short supply in Third World countries, even those rich in oil assets. The rigidly controlled socialist economies of the Soviet bloc, which fear the liberating effects of personalized communications media, are lagging as well behind the "information societies" of the West.

What Can Be Done?

Improvements in international news communication must come from several quarters. Western journalists and mass communicators can do much to improve their own effectiveness. And governments and journalists of the communications-poor, non-Western nations can do more to involve themselves in transnational news, both as senders and receivers. Finally, much can be accomplished by nations and journalists working together through international organizations to arrive at some consensus on policy questions and proposals for action.

Western Initiatives

Western media, with their greater resources, should gather and report more news of the non-Western world and do it with more understanding for the problems and concerns of those nations. The coups, the economic disasters, the civil wars, the famines, and other disasters must be reported, of course, but the press should also provide more sustained, comprehensive coverage of social and cultural aspects as well, along with more historical perspective. The public requires more general knowledge of the world so that if, say, Afghanistan or Indonesia suddenly dominates the news, readers can react more knowledgeably. People in the West would benefit from a better balanced flow of news.

Television news, still locked into a half-hour format, needs to expand its foreign coverage and, furthermore, do more than provide blanket coverage of a single big story, such as the *Challenger* explosion or the U.S. bombing of Libya, while virtually ignoring other important stories elsewhere. Television networks should revive the hour-long news documentary, which has almost disappeared from television screens.

Western media should invest more money and human resources in covering foreign news and not leave the immense task to the few media groups that do maintain correspondents abroad. And papers and broadcasters without their own reporters abroad should do a better job of using the considerable amount of foreign news available from news services and syndicates.

Foreign news editors could make much more use, as well, of academic sources. Hundreds of area specialists who have current and reliable information about every corner of the world are to be found throughout American universities. A political scientist, for example, who has just returned from a summer in Rwanda, could write an informative background story about a country rarely visited by foreign correspondents.

Programs to train journalists from abroad should be continued and expanded. Western news agencies have helped to establish national news agencies and trained personnel to run them. For years, a steady stream of journalists and broadcasters have come to Europe and America for training and internships, a fact rarely acknowledged by New World Information Order advocates.

Western media organizations should also consider selectively establishing newspapers in Third World countries. Although such a course can be fraught with political risks and accusations of "neocolonialism," some previous ventures have been successful and have markedly raised the level of journalism in those countries. Two of the best newspapers in black Africa, the *Daily Times* of Nigeria and the *Daily Nation* of Kenya were started by foreign publishers as commercial ventures. India has a number of vigorous newspapers today because British interests started newspapers there during colonial rule. After independence, these papers were taken over completely by Indians and have served that nation well.

Closer Western ties can be established between journalists of different nationalities through professional groups such as the International Press Institute, International Federation of Journalists, and the Inter American Press Association. This can only lead to better understanding of common problems and increased cooperation. These organizations and others, such as Amnesty International, often come to the aid of journalists and news media who have been victims of political repression because of their journalistic activities.

Journalists of various nations working together in professional organizations can assist the Third World in such practical matters as (1) subsidies for expensive newsprint, which is almost entirely produced in northern nations; (2) obtaining media equipment such as presses and broadcast electronics from Western media; and (3) helping to obtain cheaper, preferential rates for news transmissions via comsats, telex, and cable.

Third World Initiatives

To better balance the flow of information, the news media in the developing nations must be improved and expanded. This is the clearest conclusion of the New World Information Order controversy, but this will not be easy because any nation's mass media grow and expand along with general economic development and the modernization of individuals. Although training and technical assistance from outside can be helpful, the impetus for improvement must come from within.

A few Western news agencies and other media should not dominate global news gathering as they do, but they themselves are incapable of correcting the inequities of the system — nor should it be expected they can. Newspapers and broadcasters in Africa or South Asia should not have to rely upon a news agency based in London or New York to find out what is happening in their own region. A much greater diversity of news sources for the world's media to draw upon is needed. For that reason alone, the persistent efforts in Asia, Africa, and Latin America to establish regional news agencies and broadcasting exchange agreements should be encouraged, despite the difficulties involved.

How soon and how effectively the developing nations can improve their news media may well depend on how their governments respond to the following policy questions.

1. Will Third World nations cooperate effectively in developing regional and continental telecommunications and news exchanges?

In Africa, for example, long-distance telecommunications, including direct-broadcast satellites, can have a revolutionary potential for the sub-Sahara by providing a truly continental system of telecommunications where none has previously existed. An integrated system of regional satellites, cable systems, ground stations, improved AM and FM broadcasting, and microwave relays can have important implications for intra-African exchanges of news, educational broadcasting, telephone service, television programming, high-speed date transfers, etc. India's *Insat 1-B* regional comsat is providing an important model for such a system. Effectiveness of the Pan African News Agency would be greatly enhanced by such improved telecommunications.

2. Will Third World governments show more concern both for their own peoples' right to know and for an unimpeded flow of information throughout the world?

Too much of the world news controversy has involved the claims of professional journalists versus the rights of governments to regulate news and information. In today's world, any person, whether born in Pakistan, Norway, Peru, or Tanzania, has the right, at least in theory, to acquire information that affects his or her own welfare and future. And the government under which that person lives should respect that right. A hopeless ideal, some will say, since the overwhelming majority of the world's peoples live under authoritarianism and are far removed from information sources. Nevertheless, that is the direction in which the world must move.

To participate in global news flow requires that information, news, technical data, and cultural fare be permitted to move unimpeded across borders. It also requires that journalists be protected by law from government intrusion in their activities.

3. Will Third World nations encourage more diversity and freedom in news and information?

Regional and alternative news agencies such as the Interpress agency can be helpful and should be actively fostered. A key question is whether the governments will provide their own journalists and broadcasters greater autonomy and independence. Journalism flourishes best in an atmosphere of freedom from government and corporate interference, but few journalists in non-Western nations enjoy such latitude. Too many, unfortunately, either work for autocratic governments or are at the mercy of arbitrary political interference.

Too few governments in the world today permit their own journalists the freedom to probe serious internal problems, much less allow them to criticize even mildly the performance of those in authority. Third World and Communist nations will continue to lag behind the "information societies" of the West until they evolve into constitutional, democratic societies with free market economies. That will take time, and some nations obviously will not opt for that path to development. But to date, no Socialist nation, whether in Eastern Europe or the Third World, has shown the flexibility and dynamism to join the "information societies."

In conclusion, what has happened to international news communication in the past quarter century is, of course, only one aspect of the broad trend of the revolution in information processing that has been transforming the modern world, making it ever smaller and more interdependent. The conflicts we have seen between various concepts of journalism—Western, Developmental, Authoritarian, and Communist—as epitomized by the debate over a New World Information Order, are just aspects of broader issues of international relations.

For the foreseeable future, the system of international communication will probably maintain its present basic structure. Modifications will come mainly from the adoption of more technological innovations and not by declarations of a new "order" to end "neocolonial" control of international news. In the late twentieth century, communications technology has proved a far more powerful force for change than political ideology.

Selected Bibliography

ADAMS, WILLIAM C. *Television Coverage of International Affairs.* Norwood, N.J.: Ablex, 1982.

ALISKY, MARVIN. *Latin American Media: Guidance and Censorship.* Ames: Iowa State University Press, 1981.

ANDERSON, RAYMOND. "USSR: How Lenin's Guidelines Shape the News," *Columbia Journalism Review.* September/October 1984, pp. 40–43.

BOYD, DOUGLAS A. *Broadcasting in the Arab World.* Philadelphia: Temple University Press, 1982.

BOYD-BARRETT, OLIVER. *International News Agencies.* Beverly Hills: Sage, 1980.

BROWN, LESTER. *State of the World.* New York: W. W. Norton, 1986.

BROWNE, DONALD R. *International Radio Broadcasting: The Limits of the Limitless Medium.* New York: Praeger, 1982.

DESMOND, ROBERT. *Tides of War: World News Reporting, 1931–45.* Iowa City: University of Iowa Press, 1984.

————. *Crisis and Conflict: World News Reporting between Two Wars, 1920–40.* Iowa City: University of Iowa Press, 1982.

DIZARD, WILSON P. *The Coming Information Age.* New York: Longman, 1982.

EDELSTEIN, ALEX. *Comparative Communication Research.* Beverly Hills: Sage, 1982.

FASCELL, DANTE. *International News: Freedom under Attack.* Beverly Hills: Sage, 1979.

FISHER, GLEN. *American Communication in a Global Society.* Norwood, N.J.: Ablex, 1982.

GERBNER, GEORGE, AND MARSHA SEIFERT. *World Communications: A Handbook.* New York: Longman, 1984.

GIFFARD, C. A. "Developed and Developing Nations' News in U. S. Wire Files to Asia." *Journalism Quarterly* 61, no. 1 (Spring 1984):14–18.

———. "The Inter Press Service: New Information for a New Order." *Journalism Quarterly* 62, no. 1 (Spring 1985):17–23, 44.

HACHTEN, WILLIAM A. *Muffled Drums: The News Media in Africa.* Ames: Iowa State University Press, 1971.

HACHTEN, WILLIAM A., AND C. A. GIFFARD. *The Press and Apartheid: Repression and Propaganda in South Africa.* Madison: University of Wisconsin Press, 1984.

HAMELINK, CEES J. *Cultural Autonomy in Global Communication: Planning National Information Policy.* New York: Longman, 1983.

HEAD, SYDNEY W. *World Broadcasting Systems: A Comparative Analysis.* Belmont, Calif.: Wadsworth, 1985.

HOPKINS, MARK. *Russia's Underground Press.* New York: Praeger, 1983.

HORTON, PHILIP C. *The Third World and Press Freedom.* New York: Praeger, 1978.

HOWKINS, JOHN. *Mass Communications in China.* New York: Longman, 1982.

JOHNSON, PAUL. *Modern Times: The World from the Twenties to the Eighties.* New York: Harper and Row, 1983.

KATZ, ELIHU, AND GEORGE WEDELL. *Broadcasting in the Third World: Promise and Performance.* Cambridge: Harvard University Press, 1977.

KELLY, SEAN. *Access Denied: The Politics of Press Censorship.* Georgetown: Washington Papers, no. 55, 1978.

KRAUTHAMMER, CHARLES. "Brave News World." *New Republic,* May 14, 1981, pp. 23–25.

LEE, CHIN-CHUAN. *Media Imperialism Reconsidered.* Beverly Hills: Sage, 1980.

McPHAIL, THOMAS. *Electronic Colonialism: The Future of International Broadcasting and Communication.* Beverly Hills: Sage, 1981.

McQUAIL, DENIS. *Mass Communication Theory.* Beverly Hills: Sage, 1983.

MADDOX, BRENDA. "The Telecommunication Revolution." *World Press Review,* December 1981, pp. 22–24.

Many Voices, One World. Paris: UNESCO, 1980, 1984.

MARKEL, LESTER, AND AUDREY MARCH. *Global Challenge to the United States.* Cranbury, N.J.: Associated University Presses, 1976.

MASMOUDI, MUSTAPHA. *The New World Information Order.* Document 31, submitted to the MacBride Commission, 1978.

MEISLER, STANLEY. "Covering the Third World (or trying to)," *Columbia Journalism Review,* November/December 1978, pp. 34–38.

MERRILL, JOHN C. *Global Journalism: A Survey of the World's Mass Media.* New York: Longman, 1983.

MICKELSON, SIG. *America's Other Voice: The Story of Radio Free Europe and Radio Liberty.* New York: Praeger, 1983.

NORDENSTRENG, KAARLE. *The Mass Media Declaration of UNESCO.* Norwood, N.J.: Ablex, 1984.

POOL, ITHIEL DE SOLA. *Technologies of Freedom.* Cambridge: Belknap, 1983.

READ, WILLIAM. *America's Mass Media Merchants.* Baltimore: Johns Hopkins University Press, 1976.

RICHSTAD, JIM, AND MICHAEL ANDERSON. *Crisis in International News.* New York: Columbia University Press, 1981.

RIGHTER, ROSEMARY. *Whose News? Politics, the Press and the Third World.* New York: Times Books, 1978.

ROSENBLUM, MORT. *Coups and Earthquakes: Reporting the Third World for America.* New York: Harper and Row, 1979.

SCHILLER, HERBERT. *Information and the Crisis Economy.* Norwood, N.J.: Ablex, 1984.

SHANOR, DONALD. *Behind the Lines: The Private War against Soviet Censorship.* New York: St. Martin, 1985.

STEVENSON, ROBERT, AND DONALD SHAW. *Foreign News and the New World Information Order.* Ames: Iowa State University Press, 1984.

TUNSTALL, JEREMY. *The Media Are American: Anglo-American Media in the World.* London: Constable, 1977.

Index